HIDDEN HISTORY

of

AUGUSTA

Dr. Tom Mack

THE
History
PRESS

Published by The History Press
Charleston, SC
www.historypress.net

Copyright © 2015 by Tom Mack
All rights reserved

Cover image: Broad Street, Augusta, Georgia, 1903. *Library of Congress*.
Back cover, top: Frank Coffyn, 1911. *Library of Congress*; *bottom*: Oil painting of Sibley Mill with
Confederate obelisk-chimney, 2015. *Michael Budd, BFA*.

First published 2015

Manufactured in the United States

ISBN 978.1.62619.848.7

Library of Congress Control Number: 2015945698

Notice: The information in this book is true and complete to the best of our knowledge. It is
offered without guarantee on the part of the author or The History Press. The author and
The History Press disclaim all liability in connection with the use of this book.

CONTENTS

CONTENTS

Acknowledgements

Much of the information contained herein is the product of synthesizing a variety of sources to provide a fresh perspective on what for some Augustans may be relatively familiar tales.

All the secondary sources are listed in the bibliography; for the bulk of the original material (primary sources) used in compiling this volume, I am particularly grateful to Carol Waggoner-Angleton at the Reese Library at Georgia Regents University in Augusta. My visits to the Special Collections Department offered a number of happy discoveries, and the help provided by the professional staff, particularly in scanning vintage photographs for this volume, was particularly welcome. The Reese Library houses rich archival resources on local figures, including original manuscripts about and by Berry Benson, Edison Marshall and Berry Fleming.

As with the first two volumes in my Central Savannah River Area trilogy, I would like to thank those on my home campus at the University of South Carolina–Aiken who have gone out of their way to offer support, particularly Carol McKay of the College of Humanities and Social Sciences and Deborah Tritt at the Gregg-Graniteville Library.

Thanks also to Nicole McLeod at the Morris Museum of Art in Augusta for the scan of the marvelous Frank Millet portrait of Archibald Butt, a gift of Margaret Pepper and now part of the museum's permanent collection. The tragic fate shared by both the portraitist and his sitter adds poignancy to the painted image.

For their help in obtaining additional illustrations, I want to acknowledge Elaine McConnell, rare books curator at the United States Military Academy Library (West Point); Don Beagle, director of library services, Belmont Abbey College; Christy Foreman, library director, Father Ryan High School (Nashville); and Bryan Haltermann, president, Haltermann Partners, Inc. (Augusta).

Finally, my deepest appreciation I reserve for Michael Budd, who produced the splendid painting used on the back cover; he also took the author photo.

INTRODUCTION

This volume is the third in what might rightfully be labeled my CSRA trilogy, a three-volume exploration of the Central Savannah River Area that began with the publication in 2009 of *Circling the Savannah*, which offers an introduction to more than thirty cultural sites on both sides of the river.

To that guide, which focuses on places, have now been added two volumes that highlight key figures and moments in the history of both Aiken and Augusta. *Hidden History of Aiken County*, published in 2012, features twenty-eight chapters that cover the period from Hernando De Soto's incursion in 1540 to the renewal of one of Aiken's most glorious winter estates in 1989. Focusing on the Georgia side of the river, the present volume follows the same pattern: introducing the reader to colorful figures and pivotal events in the history of Augusta, beginning with the beleaguered princess whose name the town bears and ending with an international opera star born and raised in Augusta.

Profitable cross-referencing results when one reads all three books. The present volume, for example, contains a chapter on William Few, who often found himself at odds with another significant Augustan of the Revolutionary period, George Walton. For those readers seeking more information on Walton, there is a chapter in *Circling the Savannah*. Furthermore, in the chapter on Richard Henry Wilde contained herein, there is a reference to William Gilmore Simms; *Circling the Savannah* has a chapter devoted to the career of that nineteenth-century novelist and critic and to the fate of his South Carolina plantation.

As with my volume on Aiken County, *Hidden History of Augusta* does not pretend to provide an exhaustive study of the development of one particular southern locale. Instead, each chapter in *Hidden History of Augusta* is intended as an independent narrative, showcasing a particular figure or event; taken collectively, however, the chapters, which are arranged chronologically, can offer a selective overview of the colorful history of a singular municipality.

In essence, this particular book is yet another addition to the Hidden History series published by The History Press; some volumes in the series focus on individual towns or counties, while others cover whole states. What they have in common is the desire to expose readers to information that may not have been heretofore readily available in the public domain, hence the use of the term "hidden."

Thus, some of the chapters in this volume may cover topics completely unfamiliar to the average reader; others may offer new insights, informed by contemporary scholarship, regarding figures and events already known to those conversant with local lore. Regardless of their level of familiarity with Augusta history, however, it is my hope that all readers will find something of interest in the present volume, which compiles within a single set of covers twenty narratives that the reader will not encounter elsewhere in one book.

Chapter 1

1736: The City's Namesake Faces a Host of Challenges, Both Public and Personal

S he really had no idea what was in store for her. Princess Augusta was only seventeen when she married Frederick, Prince of Wales. What is more, she had met her betrothed, the presumptive heir to the British throne, for the first time only three days before the wedding. Like so many dynastic marriages, it had all been arranged by their parents.

Augusta was born in the German duchy of Saxe-Gotha, one of nineteen children fathered by Duke Frederick II; her future husband, also named Frederick, was twelve years her senior and the son of the British monarch George II. The latter fact makes it all the more remarkable that they married at all because George II hated his eldest son—he once called him "the greatest villain that ever was born"—and Frederick, in turn, deeply distrusted his father. In fact, when his royal progenitor set his mind on Augusta as a suitable daughter-in-law, Prince Frederick sent his own emissary to the court of Saxe-Gotha to provide him with an independent assessment. The report was sufficiently encouraging that he formally accepted his father's decision.

Thus, on April 25, 1736, Augusta landed in Greenwich, England, where she stayed at the Queen's House, the former residence of Henrietta, the unhappy consort of Charles I. Knowing no English—her mother insisted that since the Hanoverian succession, everyone in England spoke German and, therefore, no further language instruction was necessary—Augusta was more than happy to spend some time with her intended before meeting his parents and facing the public eye. Despite the fact that she may not have matched everyone's ideal of female beauty—her future mother-in-law,

Queen's House, Greenwich, designed by Inigo Jones in 1616. *Tom Mack.*

Queen Caroline, observed that Augusta had a "wretched figure," perhaps because of her short height and long arms—the young couple got along swimmingly from the first. Frederick took Augusta on a pleasure cruise on the Thames on the barge that he had built to his own specifications and that is now on display in the National Maritime Museum in Greenwich.

For the wedding in the Chapel Royal at St. James Palace, George Frederic Handel wrote an anthem entitled "Sing Unto God," based on Psalms 68, 106 and 128. That same year, a small trading post in Georgia was named for the new Princess of Wales.

Frederick himself was perhaps in as much need of a friend as was Augusta. Left to the care of others when he was only seven, he was not reunited with his parents until he was twenty-two. He had been left in Hanover when George and Caroline followed Frederick's grandfather, the prince-elector of Hanover, to London to be crowned George I of Great Britain and Ireland in 1714. In the case of this particular family unit, however, absence did not make the heart grow fonder.

No one really knows the source of the animosity that developed, more on Frederick's parents' side than on his. For his part, Frederick seems to have been, most historians agree, a congenial and approachable fellow. He liked a good time, particularly card playing and attending the races and the theater, but he was not very careful with his money. Still, in his defense, his notoriously tightfisted father kept Frederick on a short leash, appropriating for himself half of the parliamentary allowance owed to his son.

The reason for their parental antipathy may be found in the fact that George and Caroline feared that the heir to the throne was more popular than they. His mother once said, "Fritz's popularity makes me vomit." That kind of disdain would naturally drive a child to seek the comfort of those outside the family circle; in Frederick's case, he did eventually enjoy tweaking his father's nose by taking up causes that George II and his ministers found offensive. When, for example, the Gin Act of 1736 was imposed by Robert Walpole, George II's principal advisor and generally considered to be the country's first prime minister, Frederick made known his personal opposition to this attempt on the part of His Majesty's government to curb the consumption of that particular alcoholic beverage by raising a glass in a public tavern. A year later, he

Prince Frederick's barge, built in 1732, National Maritime Museum, London. *Tom Mack.*

further endeared himself to the masses when he supervised efforts to bring a fire under control in the vicinity of Temple Church in London. True to her customarily un-maternal stance, Queen Carolina doubted the veracity of the report since she claimed her son to be a "coward."

What value did Augusta bring to the union? Besides offering her husband the emotional support that his parents failed to supply, she helped to enhance his public image. There is plenty of evidence to suggest that they were a very sociable and gregarious couple—possessing much more of the "common touch" than the king and queen. Within a year of her arrival in the country, for example, Augusta spoke better English than either of her royal in-laws. At critical times over the years, she also took it upon herself to intercede on her husband's behalf, more than once prostrating herself before the royal couple in order to blunt their antagonism.

Most significantly, Augusta did her duty by producing an heir and many spares: indeed, she was pregnant with her ninth child when Frederick died unexpectedly in 1750 at the age of forty-four.

Her first pregnancy, however, is the one that has become the stuff of legend. Having been notified that their daughter-in-law was with child, the king and queen insisted that Augusta spend her period of confinement at Hampton Court Palace—for the purposes of undisputed succession, it was customary that all royal births be witnessed. Frederick, however, had other plans. He was so tired of his parents' micro-management of court life— arguments often broke out over simple matters like who was to sit where at the dinner table—that he decided he wanted them nowhere near the birth of his first child. Thus, when she first gave indication that the critical moment was near at hand on July 31, 1737, Frederick had Augusta transported to his own rooms at St. James Palace in the middle of the night. Although in great pain and bleeding heavily, Augusta endured the bumpy one-and-a-quarter-hour carriage ride just to oblige her husband. Closed for the season, their palatial destination had no bed linens, so she gave birth on a tablecloth.

Initially angry that the birth had not taken place under his roof, George II privately questioned the legitimacy of the child that Caroline called a "she-mouse"—his mother had earlier commented to members of the court that she thought her eldest son was impotent—but they eventually came to their senses and publicly proclaimed the arrival of a daughter to the Prince and Princess of Wales.

That "harmony" was not to last long.

What is the couple's legacy? For one thing, Frederick and Augusta raised a future king. Their eldest son was to become George III, born two months

Princess Augusta. *Reese Library Special Collections, Georgia Regents University, Augusta.*

premature in 1738. All evidence points to the fact that Frederick was a much better father than his had been. Both he and Augusta, in fact, were very attentive parents, encouraging the education of all their children but most especially the heir to the throne.

In 1749, just one year before his death, Frederick wrote what he labeled "Instructions for my son George, drawn by myself." Therein, he exhorted his child to be "just, humane, generous, and brave." George III was crowned when he was only twenty-two, and he reigned until he was eighty-one. History has not always been kind to George III—there's the matter of his having presided over Britain's loss of the American colonies and also the fact that he had a feeble grip on his sanity during the last ten years of his life—but modern biographers have tried to present a more balanced portrait.

Besides ensuring the continuance of the House of Hanover, Frederick and Augusta made a difference in the material culture of their nation. Some historians claim, for example, that next to Charles I, Frederick was the greatest royal patron of the arts. He certainly was an avid collector, particularly of Flemish paintings of the seventeenth century and of the work of skilled silversmiths. Most of the items he purchased during his lifetime are now part of the national patrimony.

In addition, both Frederick and Augusta loved gardens. They were especially fond of walking in the gardens of their house at Kew. Before his death, Frederick set aside nine acres of that estate for botanical research, and his widow Augusta carried on his work by expanding and enhancing the property. During her lifetime, the Chinese pagoda (designed by Sir William Chambers), orangery and ruined arch were constructed. In effect, it can be argued that the couple laid the foundation for the present-day Royal Botanical Gardens at Kew.

Finally, there is the matter of the colonial trading post that would one day become one of the great manufacturing centers of the South—Augusta, Georgia—named after a royal princess who triumphantly survived a host of challenges, both public and private.

Chapter 2

1736: The History of Early Augusta Includes a Tale of Two Joneses

According to the dictionary, "common land" or a "common" is property owned either collectively or by a single person who cedes certain rights regarding usage to a larger group. Perhaps the best known common in this country is Boston Common, which dates back to 1634. This fifty-acre tract was first used for the grazing of cattle; but by 1728, it was enclosed by railings and dedicated as a public park, perhaps the oldest such outdoor space in an urban setting.

In recent years, Boston Common has become the site of public gatherings, particularly concerts, and it is largely for the latter purpose that the civic leaders of Augusta decided to establish in 2001 their own common in the heart of the downtown area. Carved from property between Broad and Reynolds Streets, this rectangular green space was inspired by a similar central plot featured in the city's original urban plan as designed by James Edward Oglethorpe, founder of the British colony of Georgia.

"You are to lay out a town on the Savannah River to be called Augusta, to consist of forty home lots each of an acre," wrote Oglethorpe to Noble Jones in June 1736. Jones, a physician, carpenter and leader of a detachment of troops sent inland from Savannah, established the town on the relatively flat slopes west of the river and east of the sand hills that were later to form the neighborhood of Summerville. Surrounding the original forty house lots and the fort, Jones set aside a common of six hundred acres. This space was designated for the pasturing of animals, for the "convenience of air" and for future urban growth.

The statue of James Oglethorpe, Augusta Common. *Tom Mack.*

According to Oglethorpe, the settlement was to be a "great resort for the Indian trade"; it was also intended to protect British commercial interests against incursion by the French in what is now Alabama. For his own part, Oglethorpe was more worried about the Spanish in Florida. The same year that he ordered the creation of a fort in Augusta, he also ordered the building of a fortification and town on St. Simons Island. Named Fort Frederica after Frederick Louis, the Prince of Wales and husband to Princess Augusta, the fort served its intended purpose when a Spanish force invaded the region in 1742 and was repelled. Two years earlier, Oglethorpe's forces had suffered a similar fate when his siege of St. Augustine had to be abandoned due to a failure of the British fleet to support his efforts.

Fort Augusta never had to withstand an assault by the Spanish or the French, but it did stand as a symbol of the British presence. Both the fort—built by Robert Lacy, the colony's official agent to the Cherokee—and the surrounding town obtained for Oglethorpe and his fledgling colony the goodwill and support of the native population, largely thanks to the fair trade policies introduced by the Georgians. These policies, which included a prohibition against the sale of rum, did much to secure Augusta's prosperity—the town was initially composed almost exclusively of resident storekeepers and Indian traders—and to gain for Oglethorpe the help of the Native American populations in his struggle with the other colonial powers.

Unfortunately, Robert Lacy did not live long enough to find out if Oglethorpe approved of his work on the fort; he died in 1738 and was buried on his plantation near Savannah. Oglethorpe himself made his one and only visit to Augusta a year later, arriving in the fall of 1739 with a party of twenty-five men after having attended a successful powwow with Native Americans, mostly Creeks, in Coweta, southwest of present-day Atlanta. His visit to Augusta was part of a two-hundred-mile trip to secure more land for his colony and to strengthen ties with the native populations. The great man spent ten days in Augusta, during which he was greeted with a seventeen-gun salute and he heard the complaints of a Cherokee delegation about their mistreatment at the hands of certain colonial traders.

Curiously enough, James Oglethorpe also imposed an early restriction against the owning of slaves, in part because he feared that the Spanish might incite the enslaved population against their British masters and thus undermine the colony's security. By 1750, however, the antislavery statute was rendered null and void, in part because of conditions in Augusta. Many of the early residents had land on both sides of the river; on the New Windsor, South Carolina side, slavery was the order of the day, and thus it was not long before residents were using their enslaved labor on both sides of the Savannah without respect to Oglethorpe's strictures against the practice.

An interesting but significant side note to the early story of Augusta is the tale of two Joneses, both Noble and his son Noble Wimberly. The father, who became an integral part of Augusta lore because of his laying out of the town, remained loyal to the Crown; Noble Wimberly, who arrived in the New World with his parents in November 1732, eventually became an ardent Patriot. Like Oglethorpe himself, Noble Jones planned to spend only a limited time in Georgia and then return home to England; he changed his mind, however, and the family laid down roots in the New World.

Noble Jones became a great landowner. In addition to the five town lots he was assigned in Savannah, he acquired a five-hundred-acre plantation he named Wormsloe; it is now a state historic site. Most of his time was spent, however, not primarily as a planter but as a government official. He held, sometimes simultaneously, a host of positions during his long years of service, first to the colony's trustees for a period of twenty years and then to a series of royal governors for another two decades thereafter. During that forty-year period, he served as one of the colony's very first justices of the peace; a constable charged with enforcing the short-lived prohibition against importing rum and other spirits; a special agent monitoring the licensing of Indian traders; a forest ranger; a surveyor; and an architect with commissions to design forts, lighthouses and even the governor's mansion.

Both father and son served for a time in the militia. Noble, as an officer, and Noble Wimberly, as a cadet, played an active role in Oglethorpe's disastrous siege of the Spanish stronghold of St. Augustine, Florida, in the early part of the War of Jenkins's Ear. This struggle for territorial supremacy between the British and the Spanish was sparked, in part, by British outrage over the punishment for "piracy" that a Spanish boarding party meted out to a British sea captain off the Florida coast. They cut off the ear of Robert Jenkins, and when said appendage was later paraded before Parliament in a glass jar, Britain declared war on Spain.

Most historians credit the failure of Oglethorpe's siege in 1740 to the fact that the British fleet did not come to his aid as planned. Whatever the reason for this military blunder, Oglethorpe thereafter feared a Spanish counter-invasion of Georgia, and he gave his friend Noble Jones the task of commanding a scout boat with the primary assignment of detecting any signs of enemy activity. When the Spanish did mount a large-scale offensive in 1742, Jones was credited with capturing a small advance force on St. Simons Island prior to the British victory at the Battle of Bloody Marsh, which effectively put an end to the Spanish threat.

On the surface, father and son might appear to be cut from the same cloth. Noble Wimberly learned medicine from his father and considered his primary profession to be that of a physician. He also became a planter, establishing his own country seat called Lambeth near his father's at Wormsloe. Furthermore, he devoted himself to public service. During the French and Indian War, for instance, Noble Wimberly Jones was charged with building log forts to protect Augusta and its environs.

Both men were also active legislators. Noble served in the upper house of the legislature, and his son served in the lower. However, whereas his father could be counted on to support the establishment, Noble Wimberly became more and more caught up in the idea of freeing the colonies from their bond to the mother country. Although in their private lives Noble and his son retained a cordial relationship, their public stances became increasingly adversarial, particularly over the British government's unilateral imposition of taxes on their colonial dependents with the ostensible purpose of underwriting the costs of the French and Indian War (1754–63).

One could argue that the evolving patriotism of Noble Wimberly Jones mirrored that of his friend and correspondent Benjamin Franklin; since Jones was speaker of the commons and Franklin served as the colonial agent not only for Pennsylvania but also for Georgia, the two men were frequently in touch. Each became increasingly convinced over time that the only way to redress colonial grievances was to seek an absolute severance of ties to the mother country, even though, as Franklin himself confessed, the resulting war would be between "fathers, sons, brethren."

Such a dramatic rift was spared the Joneses, however, because Noble himself died in 1775, the year the Revolution began. Still, Noble Jones could not fail to worry over the fate of his son, whom the royal governor Sir James Wright (1760–76, 1779–82) called a "dark and suspicious man" who should have been more grateful to the Crown since his family "reaped more advantages from government" than any other.

Nevertheless, no reprimand from Wright nor any refusal to confirm his election as Speaker—the governor twice rejected Noble Wimberly's selection by his peers in the lower house—kept the younger Jones from following his conscience. He was prominent among the men who met at Tondee's Tavern, the breeding ground of revolutionary sentiment, in Savannah in 1774–75. After Governor Wright fled the colony for the first time in 1776, Jones served in the Provincial Congress, which in essence governed Georgia as an independent political entity until the British invasion of 1778 and the fall of Savannah.

With the re-imposition of British rule in Georgia in 1778, Noble Wimberly Jones knew that he was a marked man, so he took his family to Charleston, South Carolina, where he practiced medicine for a year and a half before the British captured that city in 1780. After accepting an initial parole from the British government, Jones was arrested along with forty other Patriots and transported, under orders from Lord Cornwallis, to St. Augustine, then under British control. Although his Georgia properties were at this time confiscated by the Crown, Jones, along with the other "prisoners," was given relative freedom in one part of the town, including permission to rent temporary quarters and keep servants.

In 1781, as a beneficiary of an exchange of prisoners, Jones was sent to Philadelphia, where he once again resumed his medical practice, aided in this objective by the kind offices of Benjamin Rush, who was for a time surgeon general of the Continental army. While Jones was a resident in the city, the Georgia Assembly elected him to the Continental Congress, and he served in that body as the colony's only representative until 1782.

Upon his return to Georgia and reelection to a scat in the legislature, Jones became quickly disillusioned by the political turmoil that he found back home. Conflicts between Upcountry and Lowcountry constituencies led to the decision to alternate legislative sessions between Savannah and Augusta; finally, in 1786, Augusta got the upper hand. While the sectional rivalry was still rife, however, the generally popular, universally respected Noble Wimberly Jones became himself the victim of the overheated political climate when, as a guest in the home of Edward Telfair in Savannah, he was attacked by a "mob" of legislators and received a sword wound.

To recuperate from his injury and to escape any further embroilment, Jones returned to Charleston. For five years he resumed his medical practice there, not returning to Savannah until 1788, when he set up a medical office with his surviving son, George. (Noble Wimberly and his wife, Sarah, had fourteen children, and he survived all but one.) Jones himself credited his amazing productivity and longevity—he reached the age of eighty-two—to the fact that he slept only three to four hours each night and his diet was largely vegetarian. His only confessed "weakness" was coffee, which he claimed "leaves no sting, hazards no virtue, and destroys no talent."

A portrait of Noble Wimberly Jones by Rembrandt Peale. *Telfair Museums, Savannah.*

At the time of his death in 1805, he was eulogized as much for his largely self-taught medical skills—"the bedside of his patients was his university"—as for his role as one of the colony's first settlers and one of the state's founding fathers. Georgia was the last colony to join the fight for liberty, but Noble Wimberly Jones, eventually hailed as the "Morning Star of Liberty," was among the first to take up the cry for freedom when Georgia finally joined the cause.

Thus, both Joneses, father and son, played a part in the early history of Augusta from the time of its founding to its emergence as a seat of government in the new republic. It might be a fitting gesture for the city to acknowledge their combined role. After all, in the middle of the "great lawn" of the new Augusta Common is a larger-than-life statue of James Oglethorpe in civilian clothing—the one in Savannah renders him in military garb—with one hand holding a scroll and the other hand grasping the hilt of his dress sword. Created by the husband-and-wife team of Jeffrey Varilla and Anna Koh-Varilla, the sculpture depicts the thirty-year-old Oglethorpe at the time that he accepted the mission set by his fellow trustees of the province of Georgia to set sail from England and establish a new colony under a charter granted by George II. Surely both Noble and Noble Wimberly Jones are fitting subjects for similar public commemoration.

Chapter 3

1776: Augusta's "Other Signer" Deserves Greater Recognition

Much ado is made of George Walton, Augusta's very own signer of the Declaration of Independence. His former home, Meadow Garden, is a house museum, and Walton himself is buried next to another Georgia signer, Lyman Hall, in a vault beneath the Signers' Monument on Greene Street.

Not nearly as much attention is paid to Augusta's "other signer," William Few, who represented Georgia at the Constitutional Convention of 1787. Even before he signed that landmark document, Few left his mark on his adopted city.

Born in Maryland in 1748 but raised from the age of ten on what was then the North Carolina frontier, Few came from farming stock; but a love of books led him to pursue a program of self-education, which resulted in his becoming a lawyer. His study of jurisprudence may have informed the family's involvement in the Regulator Movement, an organized rebellion of backcountry citizens against what they perceived as an imbalance of political and economic power that favored Lowcountry planters and the colonial government dominated by that faction. The Few family stood with their neighbors and paid a price. Following the defeat of frontier forces by the colonial militia at what is sometimes called the Battle of Alamance in 1771, Few's parents and siblings fled North Carolina, but not before Few's brother James was hanged for his complicity in the uprising and the family farm was ransacked.

Left behind in North Carolina to tie up loose ends, William Few redirected his focus to the Patriot cause, taking advantage of military training offered by a minuteman group organized in Hillsborough. He did not, however, get a chance to exploit his newfound martial expertise until he rejoined the rest of the family in the Augusta area in 1776; shortly thereafter, Few joined the Richmond County regiment under the command of his elder brother Benjamin. That unit answered the call to action in 1778 when it helped repulse an invasion of the colony by Loyalist and British regulars based in Florida. Of that battle, Few later commented, "This was the first time that I had heard the whistling of bullets and found that these terrible messengers of death lose all their terror in a few minutes." That initial "victory" may have cemented his resolve; but it was soon followed by a disastrous attempt to capitalize on the enemy's withdrawal, which ended in the loss of half of the Patriot forces before they could reach St. Augustine.

William Few. *Reese Library Special Collections, Georgia Regents University, Augusta.*

Disaster followed disaster in 1778, and the year ended with the seaborne invasion of Savannah and the eventual fall of that city into British hands. Augusta was captured soon thereafter. For the following year, the only real opposition to British control in Georgia could be found in the western part of the colony, with William Few still serving as lieutenant colonel of the Richmond County regiment, which harassed any enemy force venturing into the interior. Thus, in 1779, Few's men offered one of the very few "bright" spots in Benjamin Lincoln's disastrous siege of Savannah with a combined force of Patriot and

William Few Monument, churchyard, St. Paul's Episcopal Church, Augusta. *Tom Mack.*

French troops; the Georgia militiamen mounted a rear-guard action that saved many of the retreating Continentals.

Historians now credit the persistence and physical stamina of frontier militia units like Few's—Augusta was indeed a frontier town during this period in the country's history—with preventing the British and their Loyalist allies from consolidating their power and thereby cutting off the southern colonies from their northern compatriots.

Concurrent with his military service was Few's equally significant political activity. He served in the Georgia Assembly; negotiated treaties with Native Americans, particularly the Creeks, who threatened Augusta and its environs at that time; and exercised considerable patience as Richmond County's chief magistrate.

By 1780, he was representing Georgia in the Continental Congress, a position he held for most of the decade, dividing his time between that body and his work at the Constitutional Convention. Among his other honors was the distinction of being elected one of the new state's first U.S. senators (1789–93).

In 1799, however, William Few left Georgia. As the reason for his departure, some historians point to the fact that he acceded to his wife's wishes to relocate to New York, the place of her birth. Others argue that Few wished to escape what he characterized as "the scorching climate of Georgia" with its attendant "fevers and negro slavery, those enemies of human felicity." Given the fact that he was raised on a small farm by a Quaker father and that he had very early embraced a reverence for personal liberty, it is not surprising that William Few Jr. would find slavery problematic.

In New York just as in the South, his leadership qualities attracted the attention of the general population, and he served as a state legislator, city alderman and inspector of prisons. He died in 1828, but his story does not end there.

Few's original grave was located in the churchyard of the Dutch Reformed Church in the town of Beacon-on-the-Hudson. But in 1973, in anticipation of the country's upcoming bicentennial, the State of Georgia requested that his remains be reinterred in the city with which he is most associated: Augusta. William Few, Augusta's other signer, now rests in the churchyard of St. Paul's Episcopal Church.

Chapter 4

1806: PHYSICIAN KEEPS ALIVE THE SPIRIT OF REVOLUTION

Strong in unity, reasoned in rage:
Move on, young friends!
And happy he that perished in the strife
If for others he'd prepared the stage.

So exhorts the Polish poet Adam Mickiewicz, whose "Ode to Youth" became a revolutionary anthem in his native land. Composed in 1820, the poem saw the light of day in the form of hastily printed, informally circulated copies meant to evade the watchful eye of Russian overlords.

After the fall of Napoleon, Poland had been partitioned among the country's more powerful neighbors, with Russia gaining the lion's share, including the city of Warsaw. Polish sovereignty had been lost, but Polish identity was preserved, particularly its language, customs and arts. The poems and plays of Mickiewicz are a prime example of how one artist helped to preserve his native language through the ardor of his pen.

In this case, it proved, for a time, mightier than the sword since the poet's proclamation "Hail, Dawn of Liberty!" can be said to have inspired a whole generation of young people who felt a collective obligation to take action against their foreign occupiers. In 1830 came the so-called November Uprising or Cadet Revolution. In an attack masterminded by young officers of the Polish military, the arsenal in Warsaw was captured and thirty thousand rifles seized. At first resisted by older, more conservative elements of the Polish population, the uprising fueled by the patriotic fervor of these junior officers and their followers carried the day. What began as a largely localized rebellion soon evolved into a war between Poland and the Russian Empire.

Caught up in the idealism of the moment was a twenty-five-year-old physician from Georgia, Paul Fitzsimmons Eve. How did this young man, born in 1806 on the family plantation just six miles from Augusta, end up in the middle of a Polish revolution?

The answer lies in the quest for knowledge. After studies at Richmond Academy and what was later to become the University of Georgia in Athens, Eve earned his medical degree at the University of Pennsylvania. General practice, however, failed to keep his attention; Eve yearned to be a surgeon, and he set off for Europe in 1829 to study the latest surgical advances in London and Paris.

In the latter city, he joined other young people caught up in the so-called July Revolution, three days of street fighting that resulted in the exile of Charles X and the establishment of a constitutional monarchy. That revolutionary spark flamed up in other parts of Europe, and the July Revolution in France was followed by the November Uprising in Poland.

With the ostensible purpose of "repaying Poland for the heroic Pulaski who died during the siege of Savannah," Eve set off from Paris to Warsaw. In referencing Pulaski, Eve was memorializing the death less than thirty years before of the Polish nobleman Casimir Pulaski, who served as a general in the Continental army during the American Revolution. Leading a cavalry charge during the Battle of Savannah in 1779, Pulaski was fatally wounded.

Paul Fitzsimmons Eve had in mind Pulaski's heroic death in the cause of American independence from Britain when he volunteered to support the Poles in their struggle to free themselves from Russian rule. In addition, while in France, Eve must have come under the spell of French enthusiasm for the Polish rebellion; a popular song of the period, with words by poet Casimir Delavigne, was "La Varsovienne" or "The Song of Warsaw," with the ringing refrain: "Hey, whoever is a Pole, to your bayonets!"

Traveling for fifty-three days to reach Warsaw from Paris, Eve was assigned hospital duty upon his arrival in the Polish capital. With early Polish military successes in the field, however, the "tall American doctor" was asked to organize battlefield ambulances assigned to the command of General Karol Turno, who led the Polish cavalry.

The November Uprising of 1830 ultimately ended in the defeat of Polish forces and the fall of Warsaw in 1831. This loss proved disastrous to the Polish people because it was followed by repressive Russian measures, including the abolishment of the Polish army and the closing of Polish schools.

A portrait of Paul Fitzsimmons Eve by an unknown artist, circa 1841. *Tennessee State Library and Archives.*

What happened to Paul Fitzsimmons Eve? There are conflicting accounts. It seems most likely that his military unit retreated beyond Russian-held territory to the part of Poland then controlled by Prussia and that he was captured and interned in that country. While in camp, he contracted cholera, and that disease may have saved him from a vengeful Russian enemy. Once cured, he sailed for home in 1832.

Why did the Poles lose? Most historians blame their defeat on their lack of political unity. Older Poles were more intent on compromising with their Russian overlords; the young dreamed of full emancipation. The collapse of their collective hopes in 1831 sent approximately ten thousand Polish leaders into exile. There they joined the celebrated pianist and composer Frederick Chopin, who was already out of the country when the uprising occurred. Chopin's "Revolutionary Etude" of 1831 is his famous response to the bombardment of Warsaw that same year. He never again saw his native land.

Eve, however, did get to go home. He was elected professor of surgery at the Medical College of Georgia, a post that he held from 1832 to 1849. Other faculty positions followed in Tennessee and Missouri. Other battlefield adventures also ensued.

Eve was in Italy in 1859 to offer medical aid during the Second Italian War of Independence; in that conflict, he supported the French-Sardinian victories against Austrian forces in the Battles of Magenta and Solferino. Later, in the American Civil War, he served on the medical examination board of the Confederate army, offering active service during the Atlanta campaign. In time of war, a surgeon's expertise is critical, and Eve was ever ready to hone his skills by ministering to the wounded.

The Polish people never forgot the fact that Dr. Eve volunteered his services in their hour of need. During his lifetime, he was awarded the Golden Cross of Virtuti (Military), and on the 100th anniversary of the November Uprising, a monument to Eve's memory was erected on Greene Street in Augusta. During the dedication ceremony in 1931, the Polish

Eve House, 619 Greene Street, Augusta. *Tom Mack.*

ambassador to the United States spoke a few words about the ties that bind our country and his, including the death of Pulaski in defense of American freedom and the service of Eve in support of Polish liberty. That same year, a postage stamp emblazoned with the profile of Dr. Paul Fitzsimmons Eve was issued to commemorate the centenary of the Polish War of Independence, 1831–1931.

Chapter 5

1816: Homegrown Civil War General Lives Up to His Nickname, "The Georgia Firebrand"

Although Augusta can claim more than one native son who rose to the rank of general in the Civil War, none captured the popular imagination like William Henry Talbot Walker. Despite the fact that he did not live to see the end of that momentous military conflict, General Walker was certainly one of the most colorful figures of that period in the history of his native city and state.

Born in 1816, Walker would have undoubtedly anticipated, from a very early age, the enjoyment of a life of prominence and privilege. After all, his father, Freeman Walker, had been a mayor of the city, a state legislator and, for a brief time, a United States senator. For the first decade of his life, William Walker lived in the lap of luxury, accustomed to the seasonal pilgrimage between two residences: the family winter home in downtown Augusta and their warm-weather retreat christened Bellevue in Summerville.

All that changed in 1827, when Freeman Walker died, leaving his widow, Mary, and their five children to look to relatives for support. With money from members of the extended family, they were able to keep their Greene Street residence—a year earlier, Freeman Walker had sold his Summerville estate to the federal government as the new site of the Augusta Arsenal— and young William was able to attend Richmond Academy. As he reached young manhood, his late father's political connections also came to his aid, and Walker eventually gained admission to the U.S. Military Academy.

Small, frail and asthmatic, Walker somehow managed to survive his years at West Point, graduating in 1837 a less-than-stellar forty-sixth out of fifty in his class. Although he did fairly poorly in his academic studies, he excelled in field exercises, a pattern that some historians argue held true for most West Point undergraduates from the South prior to the War Between the States. What southern cadets often lacked in their dedication to formal study they made up for in the practical application of the concepts promulgated by their instructors.

Despite his physical limitations and his struggles in the classroom, Walker's strong will did much to help him carry the day. Another motivating factor may have been his intense pride in his "high birth." Indeed, even though his family had fallen on hard times, Walker was very sensitive to any action that he felt undermined his status, both hereditary and earned. During his subsequent military career, that personal sense of honor proved a two-edged sword: it perhaps gave him the confidence to take charge under difficult circumstances, but it also meant that he frequently clashed with others, including his superiors, if he felt that he was not given his due.

Not long after graduation from West Point, for example, Walker was posted to Florida during the Second Seminole War, a prolonged conflict resulting from Native American resistance to their forced removal from the Southeast to the Midwest. In one particular engagement, Walker suffered three wounds—one each to the leg, neck and shoulder—and still he continued to fight until he was struck again, this time in the chest. He was later retrieved from the battlefield by compatriots who thought that he was dead, but against all odds, he survived. After recuperation, Walker returned to active service, only to be told that he must serve under the command of an officer with less seniority. After he sent a formal protest to the regimental commander, Walker was placed under arrest for insubordination. The subsequent verdict of the court-martial was little more than a slap on the wrist, but Walker's intemperate response to any perceived slight was to have far graver consequences in his later career.

Walker's second baptism by fire came in the Mexican War, when he served under the command of Winfield Scott during the latter's march inland to Mexico City in 1847–48. For his bravery at the Battle of Churubusco, Walker was promoted to major. During the Battle of Molino del Rey, he was shot in the lower back; once again, his life hung in the balance, and it was months before he could walk again.

Upon his recovery, Walker returned to Augusta, where he was welcomed as a hero. A "complimentary ball" was held so that his fellow citizens could honor, according to the *Augusta Chronicle*, the city's "gallant son who has been preserved, almost by a miracle, from a soldier's grave. Green be the laurels that grace his manly brow."

Any enjoyment of Augusta's warm embrace was short-lived, however, for Walker, after his return to health, needed to report once again for active duty. With the war over, this meant a stint as a recruiting officer in Albany, New York, the hometown of his new bride. During this period, he made another notable but brief visit to his native city; in 1850, he was back in Augusta as the focus of a public ceremony in front of city hall. There, a representative of the governor presented Walker with a "sword of honor" in recognition of his gallant service in both Florida and Mexico. The ceremonial weapon was passed around to members of the crowd, who relished briefly holding in their hands the gleaming tribute. The euphoria of the occasion was dampened slightly when a sudden downpour brought the whole event to a hasty conclusion.

Another honor soon followed in the form of an unexpected offer by Jefferson Davis, then secretary of war under President Franklin Pierce. Walker was selected as the commandant of cadets at West Point. Working closely with the superintendent, who is the equivalent of a college president, the commandant is the institution's chief disciplinarian and the head of the tactics program. Traditionally, the commandant of cadets is someone who

The sword presented to General Walker by the Georgia General Assembly in 1850. *Reese Library Special Collections, Georgia Regents University, Augusta.*

has seen active service and whose conduct in the field provides a model for the students to follow.

Walker served in this post from 1854 to 1856. Although he seemed, at first, to flourish in the job, another perceived injury to his personal honor and sense of fair play brought an end to his tenure at the Academy. When Robert E. Lee left the post of superintendent to take up a cavalry command in Texas, Walker expected, as senior officer, to be granted full control of the institution. Thus, when an officer he considered to be junior in rank was appointed over him, he resigned.

For the next few years, Walker balanced time on active duty at various frontier posts with time engaged in agricultural enterprise—he had bought an interest in a four-thousand-acre plantation in Screven County south of Augusta.

It is safe to say, however, that William H.T. Walker was never happy with peacetime pursuits. He was essentially a man of action, and as storm clouds gathered in 1860 because of the anticipated election of Abraham Lincoln, he gave up his commission in what had become known as the "Old Army." In fact, Walker later claimed to be the first commissioned officer to do so in support of his native state and in opposition to what he called the "arrogant and presumptuous North." Soon thereafter, when secessionist governor Joseph E. Brown arrived in Augusta to demand the surrender of the arsenal, situated on land that Freeman Walker had once owned, his son, now in a civilian role, was part of the group accompanying the state's chief executive.

Hoping for a commission from Brown to serve in any state-based military force, Walker received an offer of a colonelcy in the Georgia state troops in February 1861 but refused an appointment at the same rank when the Confederate States formed its own provisional military force a month later. Given his past wartime experience, Walker thought that he deserved to be a general, and he found his hopes finally fulfilled when President Davis and the Confederate government moved to consolidate all military units under a unified command. After some lobbying, Walker was made a brigadier.

The *Augusta Chronicle* again commented, "It has been a source of much mortification to his many admirers that [Walker] has not sooner been placed in a position where he could be effective. It has seemed very strange, indeed, that one of our most brilliant and daring military men has been allowed to rest upon his well-earned Florida and Mexican laurels rather than be placed where he could achieve new honors."

After some wrangling with his military superiors, General Walker finally made it to the front lines in Virginia, where despite his continuing frailty—his spare frame, his asthma, his old wounds—he was ready for a fight. For a time, he was happy with the men under his command and happy to report to Joseph E. Johnston. This personal equanimity, however, was not to be sustained; after he failed to gain an expected promotion to major general, Walker shot off a letter to Judah P. Benjamin, the Confederate secretary of war, citing the "insults and indignities of the Executive" (Jefferson Davis) as the reason that he was tendering his resignation and going home to Georgia.

William H.T. Walker. *U.S. Military Academy Library, West Point.*

His action was leaked to the media, and it became a matter of considerable public controversy. Some commentators—like South Carolinian and Davis family confidante Mary Boykin Chesnut, whose *Diary from Dixie* is one of the best civilian accounts of the war—thought Walker's gesture selfish and shameful. Others, particularly in his home state where allies like Governor Brown were equally critical of the central government in Richmond, thought his resignation perfectly justified.

Indeed, Georgia welcomed its hero home, and soon he was given command of a brigade of state-based volunteers assigned to coastal defense. There he languished in relatively minor service until 1862, when General P.G.T. Beauregard, now in charge of the Department of South Carolina and Georgia and in dire need of professional officers, requested that Walker be asked to return to the Confederate army.

From that point until his death, Walker was to feature prominently in a number of desperate defensive measures. In Mississippi, he was sent to help General John Pemberton oppose the Union army's incursion into the state, but Vicksburg fell nonetheless; in Tennessee, he was sent to aid General Braxton Bragg in defense of Chattanooga, but although the latter won a tactical victory at the three-day Battle of Chickamauga, General W.T. Sherman's campaign for Atlanta continued apace.

During the Atlanta campaign, first under the overall command of Johnston and then John Bell Hood, Walker was in charge of up to four brigades, made up largely of Georgia troops. Much has been written about the largely defensive posture of the Confederate forces under Johnston. Indeed, some have claimed that Walker himself contributed to the failure of Johnston to hold back Sherman's onslaught, particularly at the Battle of Lay's Ferry Crossing, near Calhoun, Georgia, wherein Walker was said to have failed to take advantage of the opportunities presented to him.

The whole period from May 1864 to July of the same year must have been brutal, especially for a man who had always been frail. In June, for instance, Walker wrote home: "You can form no conception of the hardships and fatigues we have passed through…night marches, irregular meals, heat and dust. For a day or two we have had a respite but it is only the clouds collecting together to hurl their flashes of destruction."

Indeed, one battle followed another; in some engagements, Walker's Georgia Division was held largely in reserve, but for the most part, they were in the thick of the action. On Kennesaw Mountain, for example, Walker observed, "For nine days now, our army and the Yankee army have been four or five hundred yards apart… many of our men and officers are killed and wounded every day."

The grave site of General William H.T. Walker on the Summerville campus of Georgia Regents University, Augusta. *Tom Mack.*

Walker's own fateful hour came in July. Only a month before, he had informed an Atlanta reporter that he "had rather receive the death wound than see Atlanta surrendered without contesting every inch of ground for its possession." He got his wish on July 22 near where Glenwood Avenue crosses Sugar Creek in the eastern part of the city.

During a Confederate advance, he was shot from his horse. One soldier remembers that "Fighting Billy," as his men sometimes called him, was sitting straight in the saddle preparing to survey the field, but other accounts have him shot from the saddle as he led a charge.

His body was sent by train to Augusta, and he was buried in the Walker family plot on the grounds of the arsenal, now the Summerville campus of Georgia Regents University. A life-size figure of Walker is part of the Confederate Monument on Broad Street, dedicated in 1878; the place where he fell is also commemorated by a marker at Wilkinson Circle and Glenwood Avenue in Atlanta.

Brave and intemperate, William H.T. Walker certainly lived and died true to his sobriquet of "the Georgia Firebrand."

Chapter 6

1830: Augusta Lays Claim to Cursed Landmark

In popular folklore, the term "haunted" is generally used in reference to a place frequented by ghosts or other supernatural beings. For generations of Augusta residents, it is also an adjective used to describe a particular concrete pillar that currently rests on the corner of Fifth and Broad Streets. However, the label "haunted pillar," as applied in this case, might very well be a misnomer. Since no stories lay claim to any lingering presence of spectral forms in the vicinity of this downtown landmark, the pillar cannot technically be called "haunted." However, there is plenty of circumstantial evidence to support the argument that this column is, in the popular imagination, cursed.

Once part of the fabric of a farmers' market that spanned the width of Broad Street, the Doric-style pillar may have supported the roof of a portico at the base of a clock tower at the entrance to the complex. Constructed in 1830, the market was a significant fixture of commerce in nineteenth-century Augusta and a popular place for social interaction, particularly on the first of each month.

It is, therefore, not surprising that the two principal legends regarding the pillar—there is as yet no historical documentation to support the veracity of either tale—should involve the market's role as a gathering place of the town's citizens. According to most versions of the first story, an itinerant preacher or circuit rider called down a curse upon the market because he had either been denied permission to speak at that location or the people of Augusta had refused to build him a church so that his days of wandering might come

The haunted pillar, Fifth and Broad Streets, Augusta. *Tom Mack*.

to a close. As a consequence of his rejection, he forecast that a great wind would destroy the market except for a single column. This is the tale that became an integral part of local lore when, on February 7, 1878, a rare winter tornado set down in Augusta, barely missing Richmond Academy, which, at that time, was a military school on Telfair Street, but leveling the farmers' market except for a single pillar. The survival of that solitary column sparked fanciful conjecture.

The second pillar-related legend involves the institution of slavery in the antebellum South. A handprint on the surface of the pillar is said to be the mark of a slave chained to the column while he awaited his unhappy fate; he presumably cursed the pillar and the scene of his public ignominy. Scholars differ as to the market's popularity as a place for trafficking in human chattel. What is certainly true, however, is that the buying and selling of slaves in Augusta was not on a scale practiced in such centers as Charleston, where the old slave mart on Chalmers Street is now operated as a city museum. Regardless of the relative scale of the market's complicity in that infamous practice, there is an alternative explanation for the handprint.

Indeed, both tales can be easily debunked. Tornados are notoriously fickle in regard to their path of destruction, arbitrarily sparing one man-made structure but leveling another. As to the handprint, some claim that a twentieth-century workman repairing cracks in the column left his personal mark during the process.

Nevertheless, both of these narratives have provided fanciful fodder to generations of local residents who have told their credulous offspring about the "haunted" pillar with the added admonition that anyone who moves, attempts to destroy or even touches the landmark risks a dire consequence. To refute these final claims, there is documentation that the cursed column has been moved twice from its original location, both times because it was damaged due to traffic accidents. Each displacement of the ten-foot column, once in 1935 and again in 1958, necessitated some additional repair.

The market house, sometimes referred to as the Lower Market, was rebuilt on an even grander scale after the tornado. It was eventually demolished in 1891, largely because it had outgrown its original purpose. Only the pillar survives.

Neither damage by hapless motorists nor relocation by people intent on preserving the landmark has resulted, as far as anyone knows, in misfortune for the individuals involved. As to what might happen if someone simply touches the pillar, this is an experiment that the readers of this chapter can themselves conduct.

Chapter 7

1835: Augustan Tries to Balance the Conflicting Claims of Law and Literature

A passion for Dante can't live in the atmosphere of law and commerce," bemoaned Richard Henry Wilde, whose love of literature, especially the work of the great Italian poets, he felt could not be fully exercised because of his need to devote most of his waking hours to earning a living. Except for a European sojourn of about six years (1835–41), Wilde lacked the luxury of time, a commodity more precious perhaps than all others.

Born in Dublin, Ireland, in 1789, Wilde was only eight years old when his father brought the family to the New World, where he set up a shop in Baltimore, Maryland. Wilde's parents could not afford to provide their children with very much formal education; but as a boy, Richard did benefit briefly from private tutoring, and he loved to read. Because chronic ill health kept him home for most of his childhood, books became his constant companions.

From the age of eleven to the year he turned sixteen, Wilde worked in his father's store, selling a combination of dry goods and hardware. When the elder Wilde died in 1805, Richard followed his elder brother Michael to Augusta, "the spot where [his] hope and affections first grew."

Both brothers were attracted to the small southern town—at that time, Augusta claimed a population of around 2,500, half white and half black—because of its commercial possibilities. They themselves worked in retail until their mother and the rest of the family could settle their affairs in Baltimore and join them with the intention of setting up their own mercantile establishment. At first, finances were tight, but an inheritance from a relative and property granted by a lottery from the sale of lands formerly occupied by the Creeks—widows like Mrs. Wilde got two draws—brought some level of financial security.

Finally, Wilde could give some thought to choosing a profession, and he decided to pursue a career in law. After private study with a local attorney, he was admitted to the bar at the age of twenty. According to all accounts, Wilde seems to have made a success of his chosen career, but it was one that did not bring him much joy. His personal bliss seemed to lie in another direction, and it was during this early period in Augusta that he wrote the poem for which he is now best remembered. Inspired by the death of his brother James in a duel near Savannah in 1815, the poem is officially entitled "The Lament of the Captive," but it is better known by its first line: "My life is like the summer rose."

Though written to commemorate the loss of a brother whose life was cut tragically short, the poem, whose content is marked by the world-weariness that one finds in many of the lyrics of early Romanticism, struck a chord in readers in this country and abroad: "My life is like a summer rose that opens to the morning sky, and, ere the shades of evening close, is scattered on the ground to die."

Despite the critical and popular praise accrued from its composition—the editor of the *Augusta Chronicle* wrote that the poem was "easy and harmonious and the sentiment finely expressed"—Wilde came to realize that versification would not put food on his table and that clients did not hire their attorneys based on their lyrical gifts.

What people wanted in a lawyer was the ability to win cases, and perhaps because of his love of language, Wilde fashioned himself into a skillful orator. He also had a winning personality. Six feet tall and endowed with an expansive forehead, "bright eyes" and flowing black hair, he was said to be a great talker, "quick at repartee."

From the courtroom, Wilde set his sights on politics, eventually serving in the United States House of Representatives for two separate periods in his adult life: 1815–17 and 1825–35. At first, he seemed to relish life in the nation's capital and on the floor of Congress, which he initially described as "a vast, grand, magnificent, political amphitheater."

Wilde made political friends, such as Henry Clay, and enemies, such as Andrew Jackson, whom he characterized as a "weather-beaten old veteran rough as a nutmeg grater." It was his anti-Jackson stance in Congress that eventually led to his downfall when, in 1835, a slate of Jacksonian Democrats defeated their Whig opponents in the Georgia election. Wilde's

A portrait of Richard Henry Wilde by an unknown artist, circa 1830. *Augusta Museum of History*.

allegiance to the Whig Party, coupled with his disdain to solicit votes—he admitted to having "no passion for greetings in the market-place"—led to his political ouster.

Ironically enough, Wilde took his defeat not as a loss but as an opportunity finally to fulfill a lifelong dream of returning to Europe. In 1835, he sailed from New York to Liverpool, spending some time in London and Paris before finally settling in Florence, where, he wrote, his "eyes filled with tears." He loved that city. Thanks to some savings from his days as a lawyer and to a modicum of profit from a plantation in Florida, Wilde was able to stretch his Italian residency to 1841.

What did he do with his time? He confessed to spending three to four hours each day reading and writing. Two great projects emerged from this period in his life. First, he translated some newly discovered poems by the sixteenth-century author Torquato Tasso. Wilde published those translations in book form along with his personal speculation regarding the poet's mental illness; modern commentators think that Tasso may have been bipolar. Wilde's second big project was a biography of Dante. He struggled with this work for years, finally completing but never publishing one volume of a projected two-volume set.

While reading works by and about Dante Alighieri, Wilde was complicit in the discovery of a long-lost portrait of the author of the *Divine Comedy*. Under layers of whitewash on one wall of an office in the Bargello, which had once been a palace and then became a prison, was a portrait of Dante by his fourteenth-century contemporary the painter Giotto. The discovery of this fresco portrait caused a sensation, and Wilde was famous in Italy during his lifetime.

By 1841, however, his financial resources were depleted, and Wilde was forced to return home, but not before leaving something behind: an illegitimate son. Wilde had always been attractive to and attracted by women. Even after he married a widow somewhat older than he in 1819 and they produced three sons, Wilde still had strong attachments to other women. By the time he arrived in Italy, his wife, Caroline, had been dead about seven years, so he was free to play the field. Around 1840, he had by an unknown woman a son named Niziero, who was subsequently placed in a foundling home and later raised by an Italian sharecropper and his wife. There is no evidence that Wilde ever acknowledged the child, who himself learned that he had an American father only after Wilde's death.

Back in America, Wilde took up residence in Augusta in what he called his "hermitage on the Sand Hills." The home on Pickens Road still stands, and his wife and one of his three sons are buried somewhere on the grounds; their unmarked graves were leveled subsequent to the family's residency.

For a time, Wilde tried to continue work on his Dante biography—he even read parts of the text to William Gilmore Simms, who was at the time the leading literary figure in the South—but all evidence points to the fact that he finally abandoned the whole project around 1842. Instead, he determined to restart his law practice and reengage in Whig Party politics, but neither effort proved satisfactory. He eventually made the momentous decision to move to New Orleans, where he was welcomed as something of a celebrity. From the moment of his arrival in that city, Richard Henry Wilde was lionized by local society. He lent his support to a number of civic projects, including early efforts to establish what would eventually become Tulane University. Despite his social success and his newfound influence in the civic life of his adopted city, earning money as an attorney proved difficult.

Equally challenging were the health threats posed by the coastal cities of the American South during the nineteenth century, particularly the often fatal viral infection known as yellow fever. Despite counsel to the contrary, Wilde and his surviving sons John and William stayed in New Orleans during a particularly virulent yellow fever epidemic in 1847. Wilde was one of an estimated 2,306 city residents to succumb to the disease that year.

Wilde House, 2229 Pickens Road, Augusta. *Tom Mack.*

His body was returned to Augusta in 1854 and buried in the garden of the Pickens Road residence; over thirty years later, his remains were reburied in Magnolia Cemetery on Third Street. The poet James Ryder Randall was in attendance at the 1886 reinterment ceremony, which was hosted by the Hayne Literary Circle, whose namesake, the poet Paul Hamilton Hayne, had died that same year. Eventually, Randall himself would find his final resting place near those of Wilde and Hayne in the section of the cemetery now known as Poet's Corner.

Ten years after Wilde's reburial, the Hayne Circle erected on Greene Street an obelisk in honor of his life and work; inscribed on this memorial is the first stanza of his most famous poem, a fitting tribute to a man whose literary ambitions were derailed by life's more mundane obligations.

Chapter 8

1858: UP FROM SLAVERY, AUGUSTAN BECOMES NATIONAL RELIGIOUS LEADER

For nearly thirty-five years, from 1881 when he was hired as the school's first teacher to 1915 when he died, Booker T. Washington used his position as the "principal" of the Tuskegee Institute, a private, historically black college in Alabama, to become one of the leading spokesmen for African Americans during his lifetime and a leading authority on race relations. His influential autobiography *Up from Slavery*, published in 1901, outlined the basic trajectory of his extraordinary career. By means of his own raw talent and personal determination, Washington translated the disadvantages of his birth into a position of national prominence.

In a career that, to a great extent, mirrors Washington's, Charles T. Walker parlayed his considerable oratorical, organizational and fundraising skills to the benefit of his race both locally and across the country.

Born in 1858, Walker was the youngest member of an enslaved family that formed part of the general household of Colonel A.C. Walker, transported from the latter's plantation in Virginia to Burke County, Georgia. Young Charles never knew his father, who died just shortly before his birth, and he was raised by his widowed mother until her death when he was only eight. Thenceforth, one year after emancipation, Walker was passed from relative to relative until he reached his fifteenth year. It was then, in 1873, while he worked as a farmhand for one of his uncles, who was also a preacher, that he had a conversion experience during a three-day fast in the Georgia woods.

As a result of that moment of personal revelation, he joined the Franklin Covenant Baptist Church and sought to further his education, which consisted up to that point of only two semesters in a local school managed by the Freedmen's Bureau. In 1874, with just six dollars in his pocket, Walker entered the Augusta Institute, which specialized in the training of African American preachers. After two years of study, he got his license to evangelize.

Labeled the "boy preacher" because of his perpetually youthful appearance, Walker soon became a favorite among local congregations, so much so that he was at the age of twenty-one the concurrent pastor of four different churches in the Augusta area. To meet the demands of those four constituencies, he spent one Sunday per month at each church.

What made him so effective in the pulpit? Contemporary accounts indicate that he did not have a commanding physical presence—he was only five feet, six inches tall—and that his posture was not ideal; however, when he started to speak, everyone listened. He possessed a voice described as "orotund," and his delivery was said to be "soul-stirring." To keep the attention of his audience, Walker customarily peppered his sermons with anecdotes, including his retelling of biblical narrative and his own spin on what he read daily in the newspaper.

During his lifetime, Charles Walker was popularly known by a number of sobriquets, including the "black John the Baptist" and the "black Spurgeon." The latter was a reference to perhaps the most popular religious orator of the second half of the nineteenth century, Charles Haddon Spurgeon, who attracted enormous crowds in his native England, sometimes preaching to ten thousand people at a time.

Walker eventually came into regional and then national prominence after the founding of the Tabernacle Baptist Church, which stands today on Laney-Walker Boulevard in Augusta. To purchase the land and pay off the mortgage, he toured the northeastern United States. Walker managed his Augusta congregation for fourteen years until he was lured to New York City to take the helm at Mount Olivet Baptist Church. Even then, he retained the nominal title of pastor at Tabernacle, returning to Augusta a few times each year to conduct services. It is said that such notables as President William Howard Taft and the oil magnate John D. Rockefeller stopped by the church to hear Walker preach.

In essence, Charles T. Walker shared much of the philosophy of Booker T. Washington, who advocated the economic independence of African Americans through the pursuit of education, not only in the liberal arts but also in the technical fields. With the title of director-general, for example, Walker organized in Augusta the Negro Exposition of 1893. The purpose of this particular event was to showcase the "advancement and

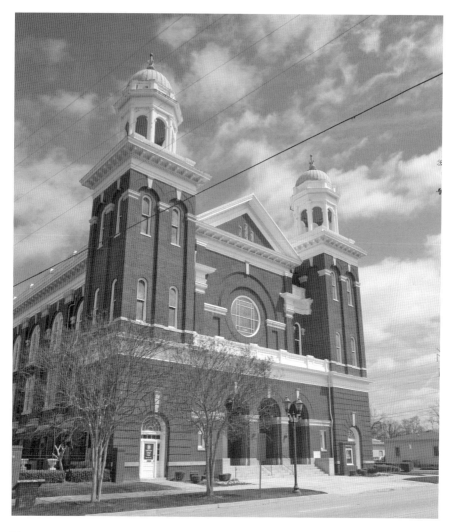

Tabernacle Baptist Church, 1223 Laney Walker Boulevard, Augusta. *Tom Mack.*

progress" of African Americans in the years since emancipation. To do so, the organizers arranged for public demonstrations involving a variety of skills, including cabinetmaking, shoemaking, masonry, tailoring, carpentry, painting and wheel-making. Walker also made Tabernacle Baptist a center for practical instruction, opening up classes in such disparate topics as sewing and auto mechanics.

Walker's many activities attracted national press coverage. His speeches in favor of tolerance at the national conventions of black Baptists in 1886 and 1889 drew praise from white southerners, who were by some in each assembly criticized as false Christians because of their racial bigotry. Here, too, Walker mirrored the thinking of Booker T. Washington, who advocated a position of non-confrontation in the public sphere.

In 1891, Walker's travels to Europe and the Middle East resulted in a popular lecture tour. Speaking on the topic of "The Holy Land: What I Saw and Heard," Walker regaled audiences at various venues in the eastern United States with his firsthand experience of places featured in the Bible, including his circumnavigating the walled city of Jerusalem and bathing with other pilgrims in the River Jordan. The subsequent publication of Walker's travel essays in a book entitled *A Colored Man Abroad* drew favorable reviews.

His growing fame and his reputation as a moderate eventually drew the attention of the White House, and President McKinley appointed him to a chaplaincy with the Ninth Immunes, so called because they were presumably "immune" to yellow fever then rampant in Cuba, which became a United States dependency as a result of the Spanish-American War. Booker T. Washington had advocated the use of black troops in that conflict since he hoped their deployment and positive performance would do much to bring about greater racial equality.

Walker spent two months in military service in Cuba in 1898 and resigned after making, he estimated, about one hundred converts. In lectures that he gave after his return home, he expressed his hope that American racial prejudice would not be exported to Cuba now that the island nation had become an American protectorate.

Like Washington, Walker toed a more conciliatory line than other African American leaders of their generation, some of whom argued for more direct political action to redress the legalized discrimination enforced in the Jim Crow South. It is of particular note, therefore, that the church that Walker founded,

The grave site of Charles T. Walker in the shadow of Tabernacle Baptist Church, Augusta. *Tom Mack.*

Tabernacle Baptist, subsequently became a significant launching pad for local activism during the civil rights movement when a series of mass meetings was held in the building for the purpose of civilian resistance to unjust laws. Dr. Martin Luther King Jr. spoke there in 1962, and the local chapter of the NAACP used church space for its strategy sessions.

Today, Tabernacle Baptist Church still stands as a testament to the vision of one man who dedicated his life to the improvement, both spiritual and economic, of his race. His final resting place is on the church grounds.

Chapter 9

1861: YANKEE TRANSPLANT DESIGNS THE CONFEDERACY'S MOST IMPRESSIVE MANUFACTURING FACILITY

L ocated on Goodrich Street just off Broad Street in downtown Augusta is a single stand-alone chimney whose "exterior dimensions were considerably enlarged" to resemble an obelisk. The base is a square tower about 35 feet high; from that platform, the modified obelisk rises another 115 feet. Its sides, as one would expect from similar structures, taper as one ascends; but contrary to expectations, the brick structure features a square cap and not the customary pyramid-shaped top. A large tablet of Italian marble inserted in its square, castellated base acknowledges that it was "conserved in honor of a fallen nation and inscribed to the memory of those who died in the Southern armies during the War Between the States."

It was Colonel George Washington Rains who suggested to the Augusta City Council that the "great chimney" with its "battlemented tower and lofty shaft" be preserved as a monument to Confederate ingenuity. What was his reason? The answer is simple: it is all that remains of the "only industrial complex built by the Confederate government."

Running a length of two miles along the Augusta Canal, the Confederate Powder Works has been called one of the great engineering marvels of its time. With buildings located one after the other in keeping with the sequence of gunpowder manufacturing, the whole plant operated like a large-scale assembly line. Its overall purpose was critical to the war effort.

"Throughout the Southern country, it was supposed that the North would not seriously oppose a secession of the States from the Federal compact," asserted Colonel Rains in an address to the Confederate Survivors'

Confederate Powder Works. *Library of Congress.*

Association of Augusta in 1882. It was that assumption, Rains contended, that accounted for the South's lack of preparedness, especially in regard to the manufacture of armament, when war became inevitable.

"The entire supply of gunpowder in the Confederacy at the beginning of the conflict," Rains reminisced, "was scarcely sufficient for one month of active operations." This was the dire situation confronting Jefferson Davis when he took office as president in 1861; he desperately needed to do something to secure gunpowder for his military forces, and Rains was given the charge to build a factory for the manufacturing of that explosive material.

Thus began one of the most remarkable success stories of the War Between the States. Indeed, the Confederate Powder Works that Rains constructed along the banks of the Augusta Canal was a miracle of productivity. In its three years of operation, it produced, on average, 7,000 pounds of gunpowder a day, with a final total of 2,750,000 pounds, enough to meet all the needs of the Confederate armed forces and still have a surplus at the end of the war. Jefferson Davis visited the powder works on one occasion and repeatedly praised the quality of its product in print both during and after the war.

Furthermore, given the dangerous nature of the work, the plant had a remarkable record of worker safety. Only four accidents were ever reported, and all those were in the early days of operation before full construction of the complex, which eventually numbered twenty-six buildings. The principal structures were separated from one another by at least one thousand feet; to minimize vibration, the walkways between each building "were covered with compressed sawdust and rubber shoes were worn by all operatives in the departments containing gunpowder." The deadliest explosion, killing seven workers inside a temporary structure set aside for granulation as well as "a sentinel outside and a boy with mule in a shed adjoining," was not the result of any failure in design or management. Instead, it was probably caused by the cast-off match of an off-duty worker whose addiction to tobacco outweighed his common sense, with tragic consequences: the deadly combination of one spark and three tons of gunpowder.

Yet despite the carelessness of this one employee, the availability of suitable workers was one of the reasons that Rains selected Augusta for the site of his gunpowder factory. Even before the war, because of the construction of the canal, the city had a manufacturing base, particularly in textile and paper production. Augusta was also an ideal site because of its central location on the Confederate map—it was thought to be relatively safe from attack, and indeed, even during General Sherman's march to the sea, the city was never invaded—as well as its available resources of water power and its access to rail transportation.

Given the task of building and operating the plant, George Washington Rains reaped most of the credit for its success. The chimney-obelisk, for example, bears a tablet that claims that "under almost insuperable difficulties [he] erected and successfully operated these Powder-Works—a bulwark of the beleaguered Confederacy." Rains certainly deserves all honor owing to him.

Yet largely ignored even to this day are the contributions of the architect who designed most of the buildings and who kept the plant running, especially in the early days when Rains himself was out of state tending to a host of other duties. That young man was C. Shaler Smith, a Yankee transplant who aligned himself with the Southern cause. Perhaps part of the reason why Smith has not received his due stems from the fact that his career took him to other states after the war—Rains remained in Augusta for nearly thirty years after the cessation of hostilities, having secured a position as a chemistry professor at the Medical College of Georgia—and he had no time to solidify his spot in the collective memory of the town's citizens.

Still, even Colonel Rains himself acknowledged the critical role that Smith played in not only implementing but also augmenting his initial concept. "In my young architect and civil engineer…I at once recognized genius of a high order," Rains said of Smith. "All know with what result, the fine taste exhibited in the massive and beautiful structures which ornamented the banks of the Augusta Canal…bore witness of his success."

Born in Pittsburgh, Pennsylvania, in 1836, Charles Shaler Smith was orphaned by the age of sixteen and thereafter raised by a grandfather who hoped that he might follow in his footsteps and study the law. However, young Shaler Smith was attracted to engineering; and in those days, the customary route to acquiring the necessary credentials in that field came from apprenticeship and not formal study. Smith worked on railroad and bridge projects in Kentucky, Tennessee and North Carolina before accepting a position at the Tredegar Iron Works in Richmond, Virginia. It was there that Rains found him.

When war clouds gathered, Smith's grandfather wrangled a commission for his grandson in the United States Army, but Smith decided to seek common cause with the Confederacy. Only twenty-five years old when he took up his duties in Augusta in 1861, Smith was to spend nearly the whole war in the city. His first responsibility was to design the buildings according to preliminary sketches provided by Rains. The main structures were built in a castellated neo-Gothic style reminiscent of the original Smithsonian Institution in Washington, D.C.; indeed, the first building to be part of that venerable repository of works of historical value is still called "the castle" (1847). He then supervised construction and thereafter tended to matters related to daily operation.

Smith also served as an officer in one of the local military groups organized to defend the city in case of invasion. His military contingent, first labeled the Augusta Sharpshooters but later officially denominated as Company G, First Regiment, Local Troops, Georgia Infantry, never saw active service in support of its original objective. Rains was awarded the rank of captain.

C. Shaler Smith (seated, second from the left), 1862. *Bryan Haltermann.*

With all of his official responsibilities, the fact that Smith found time for extracurricular pursuits might seem surprising. Described as "dashing," however, Smith made a favorable impression on the general citizenry of Augusta, particularly the young ladies. He sang in the choir of one of the city's churches and eventually courted a local girl, Mary

Gordon Gairdner, whom he married after the war ended in 1865. They honeymooned on "the hill."

His duties at the powder works continued, it is thought, until February 1865, when he was called to Charlotte, North Carolina, to rebuild a forty-eight-mile stretch of railroad track north of Winnsboro that had been destroyed by Union forces under General Sherman's command. Before he could finish this assignment, however, the war was over.

In anticipation of the financial demands of married life, Shaler Smith went into partnership with three others to create the Baltimore Bridge Company, an enterprise that flourished from 1866 to 1877. During the firm's early years, Smith constructed bridges over the Catawba and Congaree Rivers in South Carolina by using, in part, iron from discarded weaponry.

Smith eventually came to be regarded as one of America's greatest civil engineers of the nineteenth century. Perhaps his crowning achievement, in this regard, is known as the High Bridge, a railroad span across the Kentucky River near Harrodsburg; reputed to be the first cantilever bridge

The grave site of C. Shaler Smith, Summerville Cemetery, Augusta. *Tom Mack.*

in the United States, it still stands as a registered National Civil Engineering Landmark. Ironically enough, given the allegiance of its designer during the war, Smith found himself in the uncomfortable position of having to share the platform at the 1879 dedication ceremony with William Tecumseh Sherman and President Rutherford B. Hayes, who had also been a Union general.

By that time, Smith had been living with his new family—a wife and eight children—in Missouri for over a decade. He was only fifty when he died in 1886, two years after sustaining debilitating injuries as the result of a fall from a scaffold in the St. Louis Exposition Building (built in 1884 but torn down in 1907) whose acoustic design was his project. Originally buried in Missouri, Smith's remains were reinterred in the Summerville Cemetery in Augusta. The inscription on his granite monument reads as follows: "In years gone by his character stood, an example of the highest type of man. For years to come the cantilever bridge will stand [as] evidence of his genius as an engineer."

What was the fate of the buildings that he designed in Augusta? The Confederate Powder Works were eventually abandoned and subsequently auctioned off in 1872. The canal at that point was widened, and bricks from the powder works complex were used to build the Sibley Manufacturing Company, a cotton mill whose crenellated façade and corner towers are said to echo the architecture of the Confederate facility.

The distinctive chimney-obelisk was spared demolition. After an extensive renovation taking over one year and costing nearly $200,000, the chimney was rededicated in October 2010 as the "last standing portion of the only industrial complex built by the Confederate government."

Chapter 10

1865: Veteran Proves His Heroism in War and Peace

In October 1878, over ten thousand people gathered on what is now the 700 block of Broad Street in downtown Augusta to witness the dedication of one of the state's most imposing monuments to the "lost cause." Seventy-six feet tall, the memorial features a granite base with life-sized statues of four Confederate generals, one at each corner. From this substantial foundation rises a shaft of Italian marble crowned by a statue of one of the few enlisted men so honored. Sculpted from life, this figure, wearing a kepi and leaning on his rifle, is said to be the spitting image of Berry Benson, whom many sources identify as an Augustan but who was actually born on the South Carolina side of the river in the now-defunct town of Hamburg. Why was he the choice for such an honored role? It might be argued that Benson's extraordinary wartime adventures merited this commemoration. If one digs a little deeper into his biography, however, one discovers that Benson's heroic stature was augmented by moral stances that he adopted following the war and for the rest of his life.

Benson's wartime exploits are certainly the stuff of legend. At the age of seventeen, Berry Greenwood Benson enlisted in the First South Carolina Volunteer Regiment along with his sixteen-year-old brother Blackwood; both boys took the train from Hamburg to Charleston to join up just after South Carolina seceded from the Union in December 1860. Stationed first on Sullivan's Island and later on Morris Island, Benson claimed to have actually fired one shot at Fort Sumter when he manned an eight-inch Columbiad cannon in April 1861. In his subsequent memoir, he makes much ado of

Richmond County Confederate Monument, dedicated in 1878, 700 block of Broad Street, Augusta. *Tom Mack.*

the destruction of the mid-harbor fortification as a "grand spectacle with its vast column of smoke floating away."

Eventually, to complete what they thought would be their full six months of service, the Benson boys followed their regiment to Virginia, where they became valued members of Stonewall Jackson's famous "foot cavalry," first as scouts and then, after the general's death, as sharpshooters or specialized marksmen.

From the Seven Days' Battles in the summer of 1862 to Appomattox Court House in the spring of 1865, Berry Benson was in the thick of much of the combat involving the Army of Northern Virginia. Regarding his own battle-related injuries, Benson himself asserted that by the end of the war, "it was rare to see a soldier who had not at some time received a wound."

Benson himself received his personal "red badge of courage" when he was shot in the leg just above his ankle during the Battle of Chancellorsville in 1863. All in all, he claims during the war to have been struck or had his clothes "torn" by enemy fire at least eight times. Because of that first wound, he was invalided home for about five months, spending some time at a makeshift hospital in the old Eagle and Phoenix Hotel on Broad Street and then later at the home of his father, who was renting a place on Reynolds Street. Because of that medical leave, he missed the Gettysburg campaign that summer.

The next year, Benson was back in active service, participating in both the Battle of the Wilderness and the Battle of Spotsylvania Courthouse in May 1864; during the course of the latter engagement with the Army of the Potomac under the command of Ulysses S. Grant, Benson was captured by Union troops while on a scouting mission. He barely escaped summary execution as a spy. The young Benson had a habit of leaving camp and going "exploring," and his superior officers—by this time both Berry and Blackwood were sergeants—often took advantage of his natural restlessness.

Thus began undoubtedly the most exciting period of Benson's military career: his two dramatic escapes. Benson was first imprisoned at Point Lookout, Maryland, a tent city on a ten-acre rectangle on a peninsula formed by the confluence of the Chesapeake Bay and the Potomac River. The camp had been hastily set up to accommodate Confederate prisoners after the Battle of Gettysburg; for two years, a facility intended to house ten thousand men sometimes swelled to double that size. Benson escaped that camp after only two nights in captivity by swimming to Virginia—at one point during this daring nocturnal escapade he was almost hit by a passing steamer—and then proceeding by land, sleeping in the woods by day, before he was finally recaptured after seven days of freedom near Lake Accotink.

His second term of imprisonment began in the Old Capitol Prison in the District of Columbia, where, by coincidence, many of the Lincoln assassination conspirators were to be held a year later. From there he was transferred to a facility in Elmira, New York. Dubbed "Hellmira" by the inmates, the prison was one of the worst facilities of its kind; its death rate of 25 percent rivaled that of the Confederate prison camp in Andersonville, Georgia, which is estimated to be as high as 29 percent. Described by a fellow inmate as "gay, fearless, imperturbable," Benson himself joined a series of groups intent on digging a tunnel to freedom. He finally succeeded in that task on the fifth try, having helped construct a tunnel perhaps as long as sixty-six feet.

Thus began in October 1864 his second experience as a fugitive: stealing a rowboat to sail down the Susquehanna River; hopping freight trains; and walking many miles until he crossed the shoals of the Potomac, reentered the Shenandoah Valley and eventually rejoined his brother Blackwood, who was then part of the troops in defense of Petersburg, Virginia. Due to his resourcefulness, sometimes stealing provisions and sometimes hoodwinking others for clothing and supplies, Benson claimed to be better outfitted when he returned to combat than when he left.

Such pluckiness is perhaps a byproduct of youth; nevertheless, it was a trait that Benson carried through life. In December 1864, he found himself once again on furlough in Augusta, a town he described as largely "deserted, the men nearly all off in the war." By this time, residents were aware that their city had been bypassed by Union troops under the command of General William Tecumseh Sherman on his infamous March to the Sea and that Savannah was then under siege. With volunteers from Augusta, Benson left for the coastal city, hoping to come to its defense; but at that point, Savannah was already doomed.

Thus, Benson soon found himself back in Virginia. He later coined the term "camp-sick" for what he was feeling, which was not, in this case, a longing for home but a desire instead to be back with his comrades on the front. He rejoined his brother Blackwood at Petersburg, dubbed the "backdoor to Richmond." The town was then near the end of a nine-month siege during which nearly forty miles of defensive trenches had been dug. In their role as sharpshooters, the Benson boys harassed Union forces in the opposing trenches.

Lee's surrender at Appomattox hit both brothers equally hard. Neither wanted to give up his arms, so they determined to join the forces of General Joseph E. Johnston still in the field in North Carolina. That plan was foiled by Johnston's subsequent surrender about two weeks after Appomattox and so, too, was their contingent intention of following Jefferson Davis to Texas once they heard of the Confederate president's capture by Union troops the next month.

Despondent, the brothers turned their "faces homeward" to Augusta, which was by that time under federal control. Their silent homecoming after a month on the road bore no resemblance to their festive departure—no parades and no marching bands.

Benson was certainly on hand, however, in 1878 for the festive dedication of the monument featuring his statue on top; other notables in attendance included the widow of Thomas "Stonewall" Jackson, the man whose name Benson would always claim conjured up memories of the "clash and struggle of a vigorous war."

How did Benson himself spend his postwar years? He first tried his hand at being a cotton broker but eventually settled on accountancy to earn his livelihood; during the war, when he was sent to Augusta to recuperate from his leg wound, he had helped his father at night with the accounts at the bank where the latter worked. Benson had a mind for details, and for a time, he even proofread the major dictionaries of that period, correcting mistakes and notifying the publishers of his findings. Eventually, he invented his own highly profitable method for detecting mistakes in financial statements. Dubbed "Benson's Automatic Monitor: the Zero System of Detecting and Correcting Errors," his patented brainchild sold well in pamphlet form across the country.

Despite his focus on making a living and raising a family after the war, Benson's later life was not without moments of high drama. During the local strikes of textile workers in 1898–99, for example, Benson took a stand in what he saw as another "battle of humanity." In a piece printed in the *Augusta Chronicle*, Benson appealed directly to the mill owners to imagine themselves in the situation of their employees, "for no one knows, nor can he have the slightest assurance, that children or grandchildren of his may not in a little time be working in these mills for the pittance they now refuse to give." Throughout the strike, Benson stood by the workers, even providing financial support to their cause by designating some of the profits of his Zero System to "the suffering women and children of the mills" and, in some cases, helping them find alternate jobs when management decided to retaliate.

Benson family photo, Bay Street, Augusta. Berry Benson is standing second from the left. *Reese Library Special Collections, Georgia Regents University, Augusta.*

Perhaps Benson's most noteworthy intervention on behalf of what he saw as a just cause was his spirited public defense of Leo Frank. Accused of murdering teenage Mary Phagan, an employee of the National Pencil Factory in Atlanta, Frank, the manager and northern transplant, was speedily convicted in an atmosphere charged with what many saw as rabid anti-Semitism. Local political kingpin Thomas Watson, in particular, used his publications to denounce the "rich Northern Jews" who were bankrolling Frank's consecutive appeals up the judicial ladder.

Stemming possibly from his training as a bookkeeper, particularly his scrupulous attention to detail, Benson felt that he had discovered discrepancies in the arguments set forth by the prosecution. His sifting of the evidence and his personal conviction that certain facts had been overlooked or misinterpreted eventually led him to make pronouncements in the local media and engage in personal correspondence with state officials and the defendant himself. In doing so, Benson was taking a very public and perhaps very dangerous stand against majority opinion, fueled by the demagoguery of Watson, headquartered in neighboring Thomson. Indeed, after Frank was dragged from his jail cell and hanged, Watson declared "lynch law [to be] the voice of the people and therefore the voice of God." Benson, however, never shied away from a course of action that he saw as just.

Still, regardless of his public accomplishments in later life, Benson was defined and he defined himself by his experiences in the Civil War; and he continued to claim thereafter kinship with all Americans engaged in military service. In 1917, for example, he composed a marching song entitled "Johnny Over the Sea," which features the lines "We'll back the British and boost the French and take our place in the front line trench." The song itself he "affectionately and fraternally" dedicated "in all soldierly comradeship to our brave boys in France." The title page of the printed score identifies the author simply as a "sergeant of the first regiment of South Carolina Volunteers of the Army of Northern Virginia."

Chapter 11

1866: Augusta Area Offers Sanctuary to the "Poet Laureate of the South"

The scion of an old South Carolina family distinguished for its political service—two of his uncles were members of the United States Senate—Paul Hamilton Hayne lost nearly everything in the War Between the States. In fact, his small family was forced to flee his native Charleston, South Carolina, under siege by Federal troops, to settle temporarily first in Greenville and then in Edgefield and finally in a small cottage in Grovetown. There the self-styled "exile" spent the last twenty years of his life far from the glittering promise of his antebellum past but not without intellectual and emotional compensation.

Born in 1830, the bookish youngster was destined for a life of the mind. After matriculating at the Cotes Classical School, where one of his classmates was the future poet Henry Timrod, Hayne eventually graduated from the College of Charleston and then went on to study law. Literature was, however, his first love. At the age of fifteen, he published his first poem in a local newspaper, the *Charleston Courier*, and on the strength of three subsequent volumes of verse, he secured two consecutive editorial positions, first with the *Southern Literary Gazette* and then with *Russell's Magazine*. The latter publication, the brainchild of novelist William Gilmore Simms and a group of literati who met regularly in the backroom of John Russell's bookstore on King Street in Charleston, survived for three years (1857–60) before falling victim to the economic upheaval of the war years. Hayne himself described Russell's emporium as the natural "rendezvous of all the savants, the professionals, and the literati of the city."

An ardent secessionist, Hayne served at the outbreak of hostilities as aide-de-camp to Francis Pickens, South Carolina's governor and a relative on his mother's side of the family. That service lasted only four months due to the poet's chronically poor health. Hayne had, however, other uses for that particular family connection when from 1865 to early 1866, his mother, Emily; wife, Minna; and son, Willie, sought refuge with Pickens and his third wife, Lucy, in their Edgefield home, which since 1989 has been a fixture of the campus of the University of South Carolina–Aiken.

Paul Hamilton Hayne. *Reese Library Special Collections, Georgia Regents University, Augusta.*

From the beginning, there was tension between the governor and his cousin by marriage. Indeed, in one of his letters, Hayne referred to Pickens as "King Francis." Perhaps Pickens, who himself had an illustrious family tree dating back to the American Revolution, had little patience for those dependent on his charity. Furthermore, as a wealthy landowner, he may have been among those who underrated Hayne's choice of career. Indeed, Haynes himself often lamented what he perceived as a general southern indifference to the literary arts and the collective southern appraisal of poets as impractical dreamers.

This intra-family friction was undoubtedly part of the reason that Hayne himself was so desperate to establish his own independent residence after the war, a goal enhanced by his procurement of an editorial position with the *Daily Constitutionalist* in Augusta. Using money borrowed from his mother, Hayne purchased land from Dennis Redmond, a local orchardist, about sixteen miles from Augusta and built a simple, six-room cottage. He estimated that the purchase would pay for itself within a few years because of the bountiful harvest from fruit trees to be planted on his property, but that dream was never fulfilled, and even his editorial position failed to mature after eight months.

Still, Hayne and his little family—he and his wife and son took up residence in April 1866, and his mother followed suit some time later—

found comfort in their whitewashed, clapboard cottage built on a knoll in the middle of a pine forest. For furniture, the family initially used some of the boxes in which their belongings had been shipped from Charleston; and to decorate the walls, Minna cut out illustrations from some of the popular periodicals of the day. Hayne christened the place Copse Hill, and he often waxed poetic about its charms, especially since its relatively isolated location and the consequent paucity of neighbors meant that he would have to fall back on "Nature as a friend."

The copse or thicket of trees for which he named his cottage was composed mostly of pines, and Hayne himself eventually acquired the sobriquet of the "Poet of the Pines." Indeed, in his sonnets, he often extolled the "monarchal pine"; there was something about this evergreen that engendered fanciful thoughts, such as his claim in "The Fallen Pine-Cone" that he could lift a pinecone to his ear and hear "imprisoned spirits of all winds."

Nevertheless, of the many poems that he wrote after moving to Grovetown, critics claim that his most popular among southern readers may very well be his ode to the scuppernong. After eating the grape on a

Copse Hill, illustration from *Southern Life in Southern Literature*, 1917. *Thomas Cooper Library, University of South Carolina.*

September stroll through the woods, the speaker wiles away the hours with visions of mythological creatures—nymphs and fauns and satyrs—until he concludes: "The day closed whereon I drank the wine/The liquid magic of the muscadine."

The land surrounding Copse Hill remained largely uncultivated, although Minna planted flowers in the front and vegetables in the back. Because the porch was covered in jasmine and woodbine, the place must have satisfied the classic definition of "bower" as "bird cage."

From his residence enclosed in vines, Hayne would often ramble with a book in hand; as time passed, he would also sometimes ride to improve his health. For this purpose, he purchased a mare named Maggy. Hayne was, nevertheless, anything but robust. Although he claimed in his letters to friends—the Hayne correspondence numbered somewhere between six and seven hundred letters per year—that the move to Copse Hill, away from the "wretched turmoil of cities," helped prolong his life, he still suffered, at various points during his time in Georgia, either from lung hemorrhages, asthma, "nervous prostration" or a combination of the three. Ironically enough, death eventually arrived at the age of fifty-six due to a presumed stroke and not from any of the aforementioned problems.

Still, despite the challenges of marginal income and poor health, Hayne carried on. To support his small household, he took on any compositional task at hand, reviewing books—he eventually amassed a personal library of around two thousand volumes, most of them copies sent for his appraisal by a commissioning periodical—and writing poems, including verse for special occasions.

Twice, once in 1873 and again in 1879, he ventured to the North to renew ties with fellow writers and strengthen his bond with some of the leading publications of the day. He rubbed shoulders with such nineteenth-century literary lions as Henry Wadsworth Longfellow, Oliver Wendell Holmes and John Greenleaf Whittier; in fact, some of those gentlemen contributed to a fund to cover his medical expenses when he injured his ankle while stepping down from a streetcar on his first northern trip. He had to undergo two surgeries and six weeks of bed rest. His pleas for southern assistance went unheeded; only his Yankee friends came to his aid.

Yet Hayne remained a staunch sectionalist. As late as 1885, one year before his death, he was writing about how frequently he still dreamed about the "Confederate past," especially the early years when one victory followed another until the death of Stonewall Jackson and the consequent "slow, but inevitable end." He never forgave General William Tecumseh

Sherman, whom he sarcastically labeled the "gentle Generalissimo," for the loss of the Hayne family valuables when the Charleston bank where they were stored burned down during the period of Federal occupation. The poet also never understood the collective veneration of the assassinated president, what he called the "monomaniac apotheosis of Lincoln." Reconstruction was also anathema to him, and he characterized Wade Hampton and "his allies" as Christian gentlemen wresting control of South Carolina from "negro rabble, spurred on by cowardly white villains." Thus, he joined with the white majority in his native state in celebrating Hampton's election as governor in 1876 and the restoration of home rule after ten years of federal military occupation.

Hayne's vision was largely conservative. He lamented the passing of the Old South and railed against the New. Despite the fact that neighboring Augusta had established in 1886 a literary society in his name, for example, he was quick to criticize the leading citizens of that municipality, who in their rush toward industrialization had become "Yankeeized."

With other southern writers he felt the closest bond, repeatedly insisting that southern "poet-artists" needed to support one another and promote one another's work. He himself edited a posthumous edition of the poems of Henry Timrod in 1873, and he and Macon-based poet Sidney Lanier critiqued each other's manuscripts. After the death of Simms in 1870, Hayne was generally recognized as the leading literary figure of the South and certainly a leading light in his adopted state, to which he referred in 1883 as his "Second Mother."

That year, he earned perhaps his highest fee for writing a poem: $500 for the composition of an ode in honor of the sesquicentennial of the founding of Georgia. Although he did not read the work aloud at the commemorative ceremony in Savannah—it was said that public elocution put too much of a strain

Hayne Monument, Magnolia Cemetery, Augusta. *Tom Mack.*

on his throat and lungs—Hayne did occupy a place of honor on the dais near his longtime friend and erstwhile vice president of the Confederacy Alexander Stephens. Also frail and sickly most of his adult life, Stephens was dead within the year, and Haynes followed suit three years later, finding his final resting place not near his place of "pine-land solitude" but in Magnolia Cemetery in Augusta.

The monument erected on the grave site was paid for by the Hayne Literary Circle in Augusta; it is a vertical rectangle embellished with a bronze plaque depicting the angel of death. In her left hand, she holds the book of life; her right hand is raised in benediction. On the reverse side, etched in stone, is a quotation from one of Hayne's poems: "my angel of perfect love is the angel men call death."

Chapter 12

1873: Major Political Powerbroker Casts Shadow over Augusta

I was a stranger in the city, and my clothes and my manner advertised me as a raw country boy," asserted Thomas Edward Watson after his father, John, was forced to sell his farm outside Thomson, Georgia, and move the family to Augusta in 1873. A child of the agrarian South—by this time he was actually a teenager—Watson felt most comfortable in a rural environment.

Thus, he spent the next few years alternating between teaching school in the country and studying law in the city. Based on his having completed his freshman year at Mercer University in Macon, Watson was qualified to teach school, and he spent time in Screven County southeast of Augusta, instructing those with whom he felt the closest affinity: "plain, country people."

All the while, he also studied law in the office of an Augusta judge, passing the bar examination in 1875. When he started what was to become an extremely successful and lucrative practice in Thomson, Watson modeled his career after the two luminaries of the Old South whose opinions still held sway on the local scene: Robert Toombs of Washington, Georgia, and Alexander Stephens of nearby Crawfordville. Stephens, in particular, earned the young man's admiration. Despite his lifelong health issues, the former vice president of the Confederacy offered an example of perseverance that Watson could emulate if he just, in his own words, "studied thirty-six hours a day."

Small in stature but quick on the attack, Watson prospered as a defense attorney. His rhetorical gifts soon convinced others that he also had what

A photo of a young Tom Watson. *Reese Library Special Collections, Georgia Regents University, Augusta.*

it took to carve out a career in politics. Thus, Watson eventually stood as a candidate for the United States Congress from the Tenth District, which included eleven counties: ten rural and agrarian and one urban and industrial.

Thomas E. Watson, who shared Thomas Jefferson's contention that the farmer was the backbone of this country, handily carried the rural counties in his fight to unseat three-term congressman George T. Barnes; but he lost Augusta-Richmond County, where Barnes was president of the local gas company. This first election, it can be argued, set the stage for all of Watson's subsequent political activity; he stood invariably for the "little man" against "big money." In the early years, that meant taking the side of the small farmer against what he saw as the predatory lending practices of big banks—under the "lien system," farmers borrowed on the hope of a good crop—and the monopolization of land by the railroads.

In general, Watson was wary of the New South where northern capitalists had, in his opinion, won the hearts and souls of their southern counterparts, who in turn bought the dream that they, too, might one day become railroad barons and captains of industry. Rooted to the agrarian past, he railed against those of his contemporaries whom he saw as bedazzled by the "profits made by [the] Augusta mills."

In his one term as a U.S. representative, Watson fought an uphill battle, advocating such populist measures as an eight-hour workday and an investigation of the strikebreaking tactics of the Pinkerton Detective Agency hired by factory owners to keep their workers in place. His only legislative victory, one that he touted for the rest of his life, was the eventual establishment of rural free delivery. Although the idea was not his, he was the first to introduce a bill regarding the matter. Providing mail service to rural areas had been actively opposed by city merchants who benefited from the fact that farmers had to come to town to pick up their mail.

Watson's populist stance and his inability to curry favor with his legislative colleagues—during his single term in the House of Representatives, he accused his fellow lawmakers of absenteeism and drunkenness—earned him the ire of the Democratic Party establishment, which set out to deny him reelection by any means at its disposal. Thus, the 1892 congressional election in Georgia's Tenth District was marked by ballot box stuffing, brazen voter intimidation and bribery—the so-called Augusta ring was accused of paying black voters ten cents per ballot. As a consequence, Watson lost. He lost again in 1894.

That second defeat ushered in a twenty-five-year political drought, a quarter of a century during which Watson was out of public office. Yet he was far from idle. He left the Democratic Party and threw himself into national politics as a candidate of the short-lived People's Party. His involvement with that national organization reached its zenith in 1896 when the so-called Populists, principally representing beleaguered farmers in the South and Midwest, fused temporarily with the national Democratic Party. In that year's presidential campaign, William Jennings Bryan, the Democratic candidate, also got the Populist Party nomination and thus had in tow two vice presidential running mates. For that national election only, voters could choose to vote for Bryan as a Democrat and elect Arthur Sewall of Maine as his vice president or choose to elect Bryan as a Populist and elect as vice president Thomas Watson of Georgia. In the end, neither choice mattered since William McKinley was elected to our nation's highest office that year.

This decision to "fuse" parties at the national level is seen by most historians as the death knell of the People's Party, even though the group continued for some time to mount campaigns with diminishing results. In 1904 and 1908, Thomas Watson ran at the top of the national ticket. In neither campaign, however, did he win any electoral votes; in 1904, for example, he carried only nine counties, and all of those were in Georgia.

It was in his native state that Watson eventually consolidated his political power and influence. He also had his law career to resurrect and a home to build. It is one of many ironies in his long career that a longtime champion of the small farmer should himself become one of the biggest landowners in the eastern part of the state. The family seat was Hickory Hill, a Federal-style home that he bought in 1900 and spent the next four years renovating. In essence, he transformed a simple rectangular floor plan—four large rooms per floor, two each on either side of a central hallway—into a modified Latin cross by bumping out the front with an imposing portico or porch featuring massive Ionic columns and adding three thousand square feet of living space to the back.

Lavishly restored in 2004 to reflect the lifestyle of the Watson family in 1920, the house is now a showcase of Greek Revival architecture, perhaps in emulation of the architectural style of his idol Thomas Jefferson. From the grand entrance, today's visitor navigates a series of spacious, light-filled rooms featuring a host of neoclassical embellishments. The interior doorways on the first floor, for example, are framed by fluted pilasters with Ionic capitals, each crowned by a glass transom.

Hickory Hill, Thomson, Georgia. *Tom Mack.*

Hickory Hill also became the heart of a publishing empire. From there, Watson produced a number of books, including biographies of both Thomas Jefferson and Andrew Jackson, and a series of popular magazines, including *Tom Watson's Magazine* and *Watson's Jeffersonian Magazine.* Each issue of these widely circulated journals featured Watson's own lengthy diatribes on the topic of the day. Thanks to his personal charisma— he was a popular guest speaker at public events—and his periodicals, Watson carried a lot of clout with his fellow citizens and subscribers.

Indeed, for the first two decades of the twentieth century, seekers of political office in his home state would flock to his home in Thomson to seek his endorsement. Once in office, however, most politicians learned that Watson could sometimes be a very unpredictable ally. In 1906, for example, he helped get Hoke Smith elected governor of Georgia; but after the state's newly elected chief executive failed to reduce the court sentence of one of Watson's political cronies, the "Sage of Hickory Hill" turned on him and backed Smith's opponent in the next election.

Watson took his position as "king maker" very seriously, and he was not averse to using various topical issues to gain political traction and stay relevant. When Ben Tillman of South Carolina moved to disenfranchise black voters in his state in 1895, for example, Watson opposed that move; yet after the turn of the century, when Jim Crow laws gained momentum in Georgia, Watson became an ardent racist, even supporting the lynching of African Americans as a positive sign that "a sense of justice yet lives among the people."

It can also be argued that he plugged into the latent anti-Semitism of the period. He certainly fueled the flames of popular outrage when Governor John Slaton commuted the sentence of Jewish factory superintendent Leo Frank, who had been convicted of the 1913 murder of a fourteen-year-old millworker named Mary Phagan. All through the trial and subsequent to the governor's decision, Watson associated in print the Jewish businessman with the very basest tendencies of exploitative capitalism. Just as a sweet, "working-class Gentile" had been raped by a "libertine Jew," Watson argued, so, too, was the Empire State of the South ravaged by rich Jewish capitalists. Many historians cite Watson's editorials as a key factor in bringing about Leo Frank's tragic fate—even though his guilt was always in question, Frank was dragged by a mob from his prison cell and hanged.

Watson's later career was also marked by a strident paranoia regarding Roman Catholics. In the 1890s, although the highly organized bloc of Roman Catholic voters in Augusta voted against him in three successive congressional elections, Watson publicly lamented religious exploitation in the political arena. Yet when anti-immigrant groups began flexing their muscle in Georgia, Watson jumped on the bandwagon and devoted seven years' worth of editorials to a vociferous anti-Catholic crusade. His venom was so pronounced that the federal government launched a four-year investigation of the charge that he was sending obscene materials in the mail.

The alleged "obscenity" of his anti-Catholic editorials arose from the fact that he made specious accusations regarding the "sybarite" activities of priests, who, having been denied the option of marriage, which Watson considered the "conservator of morality," were free to indulge in sexual license with young women held against their will in convents by complicit nuns. So potent were Watson's diatribes that his followers helped push through the state legislature in 1915 a convent inspection bill, which gave local governments the right to search convents for "secret tunnels, dungeons" where female prisoners might be held and for evidence of infant burials, the latter the presumed byproducts of illicit unions between the clergy and their captives. Despite the fact that no proof of Watson's charges was ever found—and, indeed, the Catholic Layman's Association wrote an open letter to him, asking him to "stand up and be counted" by offering any evidence of just one young woman raped by "Roman priests"—he continued to repeat his assertions even during World War I when he ranted that the League of Nations was the pope's plot to take over the world. No one, not even the federal government, was able to hold Watson accountable for his outrageous claims. His loyal readers stuck to him through thick and thin. In a 1916 trial at the federal courthouse in Augusta, for instance, Watson was acquitted of all obscenity charges to the resounding cheers of a courtroom crowd whose leader's public suspicions about the church as an "alien, mysterious force" echoed their own.

When rebutted in print and elsewhere, Watson time and time again played the victim. In his anti-Catholic campaign, for example, he accused his opponents of trying to assassinate him: "263,000 Knights of Columbus have sworn to put me out of business." To protect his family, he told his readers, he was forced to hire private detectives and to compel his wife to buy heavy curtains to cover all the windows at Hickory Hill so that no one lurking in the bushes could get a good shot at him.

Finally, the presses at Hickory Hill were silenced for a time, not by accusations of public obscenity or the propagation of hate speech but by a charge of sedition. An

Thomas E. Watson, circa 1920. *Library of Congress.*

advocate of neutrality in World War I and an opponent of the draft, Watson was temporarily denied the use of the mails to send his publications to subscribers. This setback did not, however, stop his unrelenting criticism of what he came to call "Wilsonism."

As with many of his vendettas, Watson's dislike of his fellow southerner—Woodrow Wilson was born in Virginia but raised in Georgia and neighboring South Carolina—was personal as well as political. Some historians trace Watson's long-term antipathy toward Wilson to the fact that he thought the latter's five-volume history of the United States, published years before he entered politics, glorified New England and shortchanged the South. This was a frequent thesis of Watson's; in the preface to his 1903 biography of Thomas Jefferson, for example, Watson argues that "the greater number of books on the subject of American history and biography" either ignore the South or paint a "cruelly unjust" picture of that region of the country.

When Wilson became president and Watson unexpectedly found himself back in national office—he was elected to the U.S. Senate from Georgia in 1920 by defeating his old enemy Hoke Smith—the so-called Agrarian Rebel, as belligerent and hyperbole-driven as ever, bucked the administration at every chance.

As fate would have it, Watson's return to political office was short-lived; he died only two years into his six-year term. His followers, however, proved loyal to the end. Indeed, his funeral service at Hickory Hill in 1922 drew a crowd estimated at nearly ten thousand people.

What can be said of Thomas E. Watson in the twenty-first century? The man, both private and public, was a paradox. On the one hand, he could claim to have been a champion of the common people, but his definition of what he called "American Americans" was rather narrow. One had to be rural, white and Protestant. In his early career, he espoused progressive causes, but as he grew older, he latched onto and exploited very popular but reactionary and xenophobic political sentiments. Was he, as some saw him, an uncompromising man of principle, willing to go down to defeat in defense of his latest position? Or was he essentially an opportunist?

Ironically enough, the Watson-Brown Foundation, charged with preserving his legacy, does not appear to be restricted by its namesake's personal prejudices. Today, the foundation provides renewable scholarships to students from sixteen Georgia and South Carolina counties. When one considers that the second half of Watson's career was marked by some less-than-enlightened political positions, the fact that the foundation created to preserve his legacy now awards scholarships to deserving students, regardless of race, religion or ethnicity, is a very laudable development.

Chapter 13

1908: Augustan Becomes Self-Styled "Playmate" to Two Presidents

Born in Augusta in 1865, Archibald Butt missed out on our country's most defining conflict, the War Between the States; but his personal mettle was to be tested in other ways. Indeed, his career as both a journalist and military volunteer eventually led him to a position of influence during two presidential administrations before his life was cut short in a now-legendary maritime disaster.

After graduation from Sewanee in 1888, Butt worked as a reporter in Louisville, Kentucky, and Macon, Georgia, before taking on an assignment in Washington, D.C., as a correspondent for a syndicate of southern newspapers including the *Augusta Chronicle*. When the Spanish-American War began in 1898, he joined the army. After the conclusion of hostilities, he was assigned to the Philippines to help with the administration of that new American protectorate. Eventually, Butt's service in the Philippines and Cuba, both logistical and reportorial, attracted the attention of Theodore Roosevelt, who appointed him in 1908 as his White House military aide.

Going back to our country's first president—as commander-in-chief, George Washington appointed his own aide-de-camp—the White House military aide, what is now called the director of the White House Military Office, has had duties that are both logistical and ceremonial. Butt himself referred to his role as the "playmate or companion of the President," and that was certainly part of his list of responsibilities, particularly when Roosevelt was succeeded by William Howard Taft. Roosevelt, according to Butt, was a human "whirlwind," a man never without a plan, never at a loss for diversion. Taft, on the other hand, looked to Butt for keeping his schedule on track, monitoring his health by making sure that he got regular recreation and serving as a filter between the president and the public.

In a series of letters that he wrote during his White House years to his sister-in-law Clara, the wife of his brother Lewis, back home in Augusta, Butt provided frequently lively commentary on his playmate status. The largely "phlegmatic" Taft, Butt wrote time and time again, was always getting behind schedule; and it was up to his military aide to try to keep the business of the day from getting entirely bogged down. In essence, Butt served as Taft's sparkplug, someone on hand to activate his naturally indolent boss.

Notoriously overweight, Taft peaked at 340 pounds during his time as our nation's chief executive, and it was Butt's responsibility to "prevent him from yielding to lethargy." Indeed, Taft frequently fell asleep in public, even while sitting up, and some contemporary diagnosticians believe that he may have been suffering from sleep apnea. What were the remedies that Archibald Butt devised?

One was golf. Taft played frequently in Washington and on his travels—in his published letters, Butt wrote about a week of golf in March 1911 when the president was staying at the Bon Air Hotel in Augusta. Never much of a personal fan of the sport, Butt avowed that "the game itself is secondary to the walk around the links and the blueness of the sky and the greenness of the grass." Taft, however, was a competitive player, and Butt confessed that he sometimes flubbed a shot if he thought the president needed cheering up.

Taft also liked motoring. In a minimal sense, driving early automobiles on bumpy roads may have provided some physical exercise—at least a jarring of the internal organs. Certainly Taft enjoyed speeding with the windows down. On one memorable trip from Baltimore back to the District of Columbia, Taft and Butt presumably drove so fast that the "woodwork of the car caught fire from the heat generated by the speed."

Such outdoor recreation also included walking and horseback riding—because of Taft's excessive avoirdupois, Butt sometimes worried about the fate of the horse. Taft also enjoyed waltzing and attending plays and baseball games. The president avidly followed professional baseball and even provided legendary outfielder and native Georgian Ty Cobb lunch at the White House in May 1911.

Still, despite all of Butt's efforts, Taft was not an easy patient. The president suffered frequently from colds; at one point, his White House physician also diagnosed him with a case of gout. It was not until he left the

A portrait of Major Archibald Butt by Francis Millet, 1909. *Morris Museum of Art.*

White House in 1912 and lost up to eighty pounds that some of Taft's more serious symptoms dissipated.

Yet getting Taft to exercise was not Butt's only goal as the president's playmate; he also had to try to maintain the morale of the chief executive. That became a more difficult task when it became increasingly clear that Taft and his mentor Teddy Roosevelt were drifting further and further apart. Declining to run for a second full term—he finished McKinley's unexpired term and one of his own—Roosevelt picked Taft as his progressive successor. However, for a variety of reasons, including a difference in personal style, the bond between the two men came undone.

Some historians theorize that Taft lacked the political savvy of his predecessor; he once admitted to his military aide, for example, "I have made up my mind to one thing, Archie: that I will not play a part for popularity. If the people do not approve of me or my administration after they have had time to know me, then I shall not let it worry me and I most certainly shall not change my method." Taft also lacked Roosevelt's lust for publicity; the latter, aggressive and talkative, was adept at crafting his own legend, while the former was more deliberative and reserved.

Butt, who admired both men equally, confessed that "Taft can't be compared to Roosevelt; they are as widely separated as Augusta, Georgia, and Augusta, Maine." Still, it pained him when, in early 1912, Theodore Roosevelt decided to challenge Taft for the Republican nomination. At the time, Butt was all set to take a well-earned vacation to Europe, accompanying his friend the painter Frank Millet to Rome. But when Roosevelt declared his candidacy, Butt abruptly canceled his plans, not wanting to, in his words, "feel like a quitter in going." Archie Butt felt that he owed too much to Taft, but the president insisted that he go ahead with his trip since, it was assumed, his military aide would still be back in the country in time to help him fight for the nomination.

That decision sealed Butt's fate, for on his return voyage to America, he booked passage on the RMS *Titanic*, which sank in the early morning hours of April 15, 1912. According to eyewitness accounts, Butt took charge of some of the evacuation procedures after the ship struck an iceberg, helping to ensure that women and children were placed in available lifeboats and that general order was maintained.

Butt's remains were never found (Millet's were), but a memorial service in his honor was held the next month in the opera house in Augusta. President Taft gave the eulogy, extolling Butt's life of self-sacrifice. Asserting that

Butt Bridge, Fifteenth Street,
Augusta. *Tom Mack.*

"he had become as a son or a brother," Taft went on to claim that Butt's "forgetfulness of self had become a part of his nature."

Two years later, the Butt Bridge spanning the Augusta Canal at Fifteenth Street was constructed as his memorial; it may very well be the first permanent monument dedicated to a victim of the *Titanic* tragedy. Once again, William Howard Taft, now out of office, came to Augusta to pay tribute to his personal friend. "After I heard that part of the ship's company had gone down," Taft avowed, "I knew that he would certainly remain on deck until every duty had been performed."

Made of stone, the white, hump-backed bridge features four tall pillars, each topped with a bronze-banded globe illuminated by an electric light and crowned with an eagle whose wings are unfurled. Rearing lions holding shields greet motorists at both ends.

The bridge was designed by New York architect William Henry Deacy, who is also credited with creating the Romanesque bell tower at North Carolina State University, dedicated to the memory of the school's alumni killed in the First World War.

In the center on each side of the span are bronze plaques. One features a bas relief portrait of Butt in full dress uniform, and the other commemorates the dedication ceremony and quotes President Taft: "In memory of his noble and lovable qualities as a man, his courage and his high sense of duty as a soldier, his loyalty and efficiency as a public servant, his fellow citizens of Augusta dedicate this bridge."

In the 1980s and '90s, the bridge was threatened with destruction, and a Butt Memorial Bridge Legal Defense Fund was established, with the support of Hollywood director James Cameron, whose blockbuster film *Titanic* premiered in 1997. The film's stars Leonardo DiCaprio and Kate Winslet also joined in the collective preservation effort.

Eventually, a revised federal project spared this historic structure and reduced traffic congestion on Fifteenth Street by building a new bridge to cross the canal not far from the Butt span. Tall enough to permit the passage of canalboats underneath, the new bridge crosses the canal between Walton Way on one side and the Enterprise Mill on the other. Its arches mimic the profile of the Butt Bridge so that both structures complement each other. Rarely do highway projects display much sensitivity to historical preservation, but this project appears to be a rare exception.

Chapter 14

1910: WRIGHT BROTHERS ESTABLISH
A FLYING SCHOOL IN AUGUSTA

On December 17, 1903, near the town of Kitty Hawk on the Outer Banks of North Carolina, the Wright brothers made history when Orville Wright, on the fourth attempt of the day, achieved the first sustained flight of a powered, heavier-than-air craft. For a variety of reasons, their legendary feat went unheralded at the time, but eventually these two bicycle makers from Dayton, Ohio, were to enter the international spotlight.

Only four years earlier, Wilbur Wright had written to the Smithsonian asking for research materials. "I am an enthusiast, but not a crank," he assured that venerable institution. He and his younger brother Orville simply wanted to begin their study of aeronautics in a systematic way by first learning as much as they could about what had already been learned. By 1906, the bachelor brothers were ready to patent all that they had achieved and thereafter defend their patent from infringement.

In time, even Augusta figured in their remarkable history. From 1910 to 1916, the brothers ran what was called the Wright Flying School, first in Montgomery, Alabama, and then in their hometown of Dayton. They even opened a branch in Augusta in 1911 just off Wrightsboro Road.

The head of the new school was Frank Trenholm Coffyn, a Charleston, South Carolina native who was trained by Wilbur Wright in Dayton, Ohio. "Well, Frank, you come out to Dayton in about a month," said Wright to Coffyn after the latter expressed his interest in manned flight following a public display of one of the brothers' new aeroplanes. "We'll see how we like one another."

Orville and Wilbur Wright with their sister Katherine. *Library of Congress.*

Apparently they got along fine, and it was not long before Coffyn became one of the original members of the Wright Exhibition Team, traveling the country to demonstrate the workings of the company's remarkable flying machines. Early aviation was a dangerous business. In fact, five of the nine aviators who composed the original team died in crashes between 1910 and 1911. Coffyn was one of the lucky ones. He not only survived but went on to carve his own place in aviation history. During the year that he spent in Augusta, for example, Coffyn set a world record by flying his first wife, Louise, to Aiken for breakfast, covering twenty-eight miles in about forty minutes. The *Knoxville Journal and Tribune* referred to this feat as the longest flight by a woman up to that date.

What was training like at the Wright Flying School? An early advertisement touted, "Learning to fly at the Wright School is as simple as learning to drive an automobile. All instruction machines are equipped with dual controls. The pupil takes the same seat he will always occupy and from the starting of the motor follows every movement of the instructor in getting underway, rising in the air, maneuvering, and finally landing, until these operations become instinctive. Gradually the pilot gives the actual control to the pupil while in the air until he is capable of handling the machine under every condition of flight. Instruction and practice is then continued until the student can leave and land with perfect assurance." In essence, Wilbur Wright felt that all one needed was about three hours of training before he was ready to attempt a solo flight.

Coffyn left the Wright Company after one year in Augusta and went on to set a number of records as an independent aviator. He is credited, for example, with flying the plane from which the first aerial film was made when he flew over New York City and under the Brooklyn Bridge in 1912 in a specially designed hydroplane with aluminum pontoons. In passing under the bridge, it is reported, he flew just fifteen feet below the roadway and not far above the surface of the East River; in fact, he later asserted that he could feel the blast from the smokestack of a tugboat. That series of fifteen-minute flights that he undertook during February 1912 resulted in about one thousand feet of film for the Vitagraph Company and many still photographs snapped by his passenger Adrian Duff, who worked for the American Press Association (APA).

During World War I, Coffyn served as a flight instructor for the army; in the 1920s, his good looks landed him an occasional small part in silent films, including *Ransom's Folly*, which also featured his second wife, the actress Pauline Neff. In this 1926 motion picture based on a short story by Richard Harding Davis and set on an army post, Coffyn played the camp commandant. Despite his short-lived interest in film work—his career in films lasted about as long as his second marriage, from 1920

Frank Coffyn, 1911. *Library of Congress.*

to 1928—Coffyn never abandoned his love of flight; before his death in 1960, he had transferred his primary interest to helicopters.

Even with the departure of Coffyn, however, the Wright brothers maintained an interest in Augusta for a few years more. Thanks to their suggestion, for example, the U.S. Army Signal Corps opened an aviation school in Augusta during two consecutive winters. The military's principal flight training program was initially headquartered in College Park, Maryland, but the milder southern winters led those in charge to try Augusta for half the year (1911 and 1912). Orville Wright himself made at least one visit to the Army Aviation School—he held the rank of major in the Aviation Section of the Signal Officers Reserve Corps—to investigate losses in engine power in the Wright-built planes that the military used for training purposes.

Although the army eventually moved its permanent program to San Diego, the Wright Company revived its civilian flying school in Augusta in 1915–16 only to shut down that operation at the advent of America's entry into World War I.

Thus, for a brief period, Augusta played a part in aviation history. What happened to the Wright brothers themselves? Wilbur lived long enough to travel to Europe and amaze foreign audiences in the first major demonstrations of the Wright aeroplane in 1908; tragically, he died of typhoid fever in 1912 at the age of forty-five.

"He will always be my hero," said Coffyn of the man who taught him to fly. To Frank Coffyn, Wilbur Wright would remain a romantic figure: a "tall, raw-boned man with keen eyes dominating sharply chiseled features aptly suggesting the brooding alertness of the eagle."

Coffyn never quite warmed up to Orville, who put most of his energy into building the Wright Company, which he sold in 1915. "Distant" is how Coffyn described Orville Wright, who died a wealthy and honored man in 1948. Yet despite his preference for one brother over the other, Coffyn summed up his experience with those two aviation pioneers thusly: "I trust that we will never lose sight of the fact that it was Wilbur and Orville Wright who made possible man's conquest of the air."

Chapter 15

1911: GREAT AMERICAN EPIC POEM HAS AUGUSTA ROOTS

Although he was born in Pennsylvania and grew up mostly in New York and California, the four years that Stephen Vincent Benet spent in Augusta made an indelible mark on his poetic career. In fact, it can be argued that this brief residency informs much of the author's masterwork, the epic poem *John Brown's Body*.

Why was the majority of Benet's early life so peripatetic? The answer lies in the fact that he grew up in a military family—his paternal grandfather was a brigadier general and his father a colonel, both career officers and specialists in ordnance—and promotion almost always involves reposting. When asked how he felt about relocating from the comforts of the Benicia Arsenal in California to the as-yet-unfamiliar South, for example, Benet later wrote, "The move hardly upset me at all—I was used to moving, being an army child."

Indeed, forced relocation had become a fact of life for the Benet family, who quickly adjusted to the fact that their patriarch Colonel J. Walker Benet had now been given command of the Augusta Arsenal in 1911 and that they must occupy what was then the Commandant's House.

The new family home, a two-story Federal-style residence featuring a two-tiered portico with Tuscan columns, still stands in the heart of the Summerville campus of Georgia Regents University. Now the building serves as a welcome center of sorts, but in the early part of the last century, it was the scene of cozy domestic activity. Colonel Benet was fond of reading, and so were his three children: William Rose, Laura and Stephen. They

Benet House, Summerville campus of Georgia Regents University, Augusta. *Tom Mack.*

were also partial to parlor games featuring the members of their tight family circle. Benet later commented on the fact that his parents and siblings drew upon their own resources for amusement, mindful as they were of the "line of cleavage between [them] and the civilian rest of the world."

Colonel Benet also liked to engage his children in intellectual debate, and he was especially attracted to the decisive moments in our nation's history. The arsenal lent itself to such rumination since its first incarnation on the Georgia side of the Savannah River dated back to 1735 and the very earliest days of settlement in Augusta. Because swamp fever wiped out nearly half the garrison in 1826, the commanding officer at the time decided to relocate the facility, which was then a manufacturing center for cartridges and powder, to a presumably more salubrious setting. He chose the village of Summerville, now a part of Augusta known popularly as "the hill," where higher ground meant, it was thought, drier living conditions.

Thus, with its long-standing reputation as a hospitable refuge for civilian and soldier alike, Summerville was steeped in the past, particularly what Stephen Benet himself came to call the "frozen residuum" of the antebellum

South. The natives, for example, were still talking during the Benet family residency about General Sherman's march to the sea some fifty years earlier and touting the popular legend of his bypassing Augusta because of his lingering affection for an old dance partner. While it is true that he spent about three months at the arsenal as a popular young officer in 1844, the reason that William Tecumseh Sherman "spared" Augusta in 1864 had more to do with logistics than sentiment. His primary goal was to take Savannah as speedily as possible and to cut Georgia in half in the process.

Still, there was enough local history to keep a bookish father and his equally bookish son, both avid Civil War buffs, happy for hours on end, discussing their respective day's reading. Because of his prodigious speed—he was reported to read a book a day—and his powers of retention, the young Benet had an inflated reputation for studiousness. That image was enhanced by his custom of riding his bicycle with one hand grasping the handlebar and the other holding a book. Furthermore, an early bout with scarlet fever had weakened his eyes and necessitated the wearing of corrective lenses. A "timid, fattish, and very spectacled" teenager, as Benet described himself, would have, one would assume, stood out in the military environment in which he found himself.

Luckily for Benet, however, he found a place where his talents could thrive. Before Summerville became part of Augusta in 1912, it was known far and wide for the high reputation of its local educational institutions, particularly the Summerville Academy, which young Benet attended to prepare for college. It was there that he impressed the staff—the male principal and the four female teachers—and won a number of prizes for his studies. While matriculating at the school, he also, at the tender age of sixteen, published his first poem in a professional periodical, the *New Republic*. Entitled "The Winged Man," the piece about Icarus and his flight too close to the sun came ironically to prefigure young Benet's own faltering progress toward adulthood.

With his heart set on gaining admission to Yale, Benet disappointed his family and himself by failing to pass the entrance exams on his first attempt—apparently the school in Summerville was not nearly as competitive as local boosters were wont to claim. However, Benet eventually was allowed to retake certain sections of the test in both Latin and math. Tutored in those two subjects privately in Augusta during July and August 1915, Benet passed the exam on his second attempt and entered the freshman class at Yale in the fall.

Off to college, Benet never looked back. It is, however, my personal theory, one corroborated by a close reading of the text, that the poet's time in Augusta significantly shaped the volume that established his principal

Summerville Academy. *Reese Library Special Collections, Georgia Regents University, Augusta.*

claim to fame, the American epic poem *John Brown's Body*. Not only was this particular work a critical success—it won the Pulitzer Prize in 1929—but it also acquired a popular readership after being chosen as a Book-of-the-Month Club selection.

Covering fifteen thousand lines, the poem traces the course of the War Between the States from John Brown's raid on Harpers Ferry to Robert E. Lee's surrender at Appomattox. The poet's realistic accounts of some of the major battles of the war match the descriptions he culled from his father's library of military history.

In addition to the major historical figures that inhabit his text—from Abraham Lincoln and Ulysses Grant to Jefferson Davis and Stonewall Jackson—Benet included two legendary Georgians, both of whom served in the Confederate cabinet and subsequently cast long shadows over public affairs in the Augusta area. One was Robert Toombs of nearby Washington, Georgia, whom Benet describes in his poem as "tall, laughing, restless" and "hard to manage"; Toombs served only a few months as the secretary of state under Davis, against whom he railed during most of the war. The other is Alexander Stephens from Crawfordville, whom Benet characterizes as "ailingly austere" but endowed with a "crippled charm"; Stephens, who suffered from a fragile constitution most of his life, was vice president of the Confederate States.

Mixed in with these national and regional figures are characters of Benet's own invention, particularly two young men who stand for the Northern and Southern soldier, respectively, Jack Ellyat of Connecticut and Clay Wingate of Georgia.

Wingate might very well be a composite of some of the classmates that Benet knew in Augusta, and Wingate Hall with its "white-pillared porch," the ancestral home of his make-believe Confederate, might have been inspired by the Commandant's House at the arsenal. Indeed, there hangs about the Wingate homestead much of the atmosphere that Benet must have remembered from his boyhood on "the hill": "This was his Georgia, this his share/Of pine and river and sleepy air/Of summer thunder and winter rain/That spills bright tears on the window-pane."

Wingate, the quintessential Southern aristocrat whose family's land grant dates back to the time of Charles II, is torn between duty and personal inclination, and that tension is embodied in his romantic life. Although he finds himself attracted to Sally Dupré, the offspring of a high-born mother who married beneath her class—she fell for a "profligate dancing master"—Wingate succumbs to social pressure and pays court instead to the frivolous Lucy Weatherby, who may very well be Benet's veiled reference to Lucy Pickens, the Edgefield County resident who for a time carried the title "Queen of the Confederacy." Lucy was the third wife of South Carolina governor Francis Pickens, and just like Lucy Weatherby, she impressed some of her contemporaries, most notably Mary Boykin Chesnut, whose *A Diary from Dixie* is one of the best civilian accounts of the war years, as "silly and affected." Chesnut claimed that Lucy Pickens was fond of "looking love into the eyes of the men at every glance." Benet's Lucy Weatherby spends most of her time in the poem trying to decide which gown to wear to the next ball and which new male acquaintance she might flirt with next. In the poem, she considered herself "engaged" not only to Wingate but to another man as well. Another link between each Lucy is their shared, informal review of Southern troops as they prepared to go off to war. An engraving published in an issue of the *Leslie Illustrated Newspaper* in 1861 shows Lucy Pickens inspecting the men of the Holcombe Legion, which bore her maiden name; in Benet's poem, Lucy Weatherby calls out "brave words to the soldiers" as she transfers a "knot of bright ribbons" from her bodice to the military standard of Wingate's Black Horse Troop.

The Yankee antagonist, Jack Ellyat, also has his romantic entanglement. Following his capture during the Battle of Bull Run, he escapes to find sanctuary in an isolated Tennessee farmhouse, where he initiates a brief liaison with the plucky Melora Vilas. After Ellyat returns to active duty, Melora finds herself pregnant; she not only determines to keep the child but also sets off to find the father. As the poem ends, Melora reaches the Connecticut town where the Ellyat family lives; and her lover, scarred inside and out, imagines a future for them both in the American West. Also in

Stephen Vincent Benet. *Yale Collection of American Literature, Beinecke Rare Book and Manuscript Library.*

the poem's conclusion, the high-born Wingate survives the war to hobble home to Sally—the unregenerate Lucy Weatherby having fled to Canada—and start their lives anew on more equal footing, Wingate Hall and Clay's patrimony having been destroyed by Sherman's troops.

In extending its depiction of Southern society to include significant portrayals of two fictional African Americans, Benet's narrative poem spends time not only "upstairs" but also "downstairs." One is the fugitive slave Slade, who finds freedom as a hired man in the North; the other is a loyal Wingate family retainer, the butler Cudjo, who is inextricably tied to the Southern landscape and the "planted earth" of Georgia. While the "rough-bearded" William Tecumseh Sherman, whom Benet further describes as "nervous, explosive, passionate," invades the state on his destructive march to the sea, the faithful Cudjo is seen burying the family silver and luxuriating in his memories of good times in the Wingate household.

In addition to poetry, Benet tried his hand at fiction, and his tale entitled "The Devil and Daniel Webster" not only won the O. Henry Prize for the best American short story of 1936 but also became the basis of an operetta in 1939 and a motion picture initially entitled *All That Money Can Buy* in 1942. Benet is credited with co-adapting his own text for the big screen.

Stephen Vincent Benet died at the age of forty-four, presumably worn out by his work for the Writers War Board in support of Allied efforts in World War II. He had long suffered from ill health, including arthritis of the spine, but before his untimely death by heart attack in 1943, Benet managed to pen some of the most popular and influential works produced in this country in the first half of the twentieth century. One of those works, local residents can justifiably claim, drew its inspiration from the poet's memories of a four-year residency as a teenager in Augusta: "wherever the winds of Georgia run, it smells of peaches long in the sun."

Chapter 16

1913: Augusta Memorializes the Art of Poetry

Rivaling Savannah's park-like boulevards in both longevity and length, Greene Street in Augusta is punctuated with monuments, many of which date back to the nineteenth century. Among those memorials that grace the central median is a four-sided miniature Greek temple dedicated to four poets who lived and worked in Georgia.

Undoubtedly the most notable poet commemorated on this neoclassical monument, erected in 1913 between Seventh and Eighth Streets, is Sidney Lanier, whose works are still often included in the standard anthologies of American literature. A native of Macon who spent time in a Federal prison camp after he was captured on a Confederate blockade runner in 1864, Lanier is most remembered for poems that speak of the regeneration of the American South after the war.

His most celebrated poem, "The Marshes of Glynn," for example, is set, as the title indicates, in the salt marshes of Glynn County on the coast of Georgia. Lanier depicts these wetlands as an intermediate region between the earth and the sea. As such, they embody the regenerative and reconciling powers of nature and, in so doing, offer hope for the individual—in this case, the southerner seeking consolation in defeat—who may yet learn to win "good out of infinite pain and sight out of blindness and purity out of a stain." This quotation is etched on one side of the Greene Street monument.

Visitors to Macon can still visit the cottage where Lanier was born; the residence is now a house museum operated by the Historic Macon Foundation. A guided tour of the property affords an appropriate

Poets Monument, 700 block of Greene Street, Augusta. *Tom Mack.*

introduction to the poet's life and work, both in poetry and music—Lanier played the flute in the Peabody Symphony Orchestra in Baltimore and wrote a cantata for the Centennial Exposition in 1876.

Another poet who sought to offer consolation and inspiration to his readers was Abram Ryan, the "Poet-Priest of the Confederacy." Born in 1838 on a plantation near Hagerstown, Maryland, Ryan has more significant ties to Augusta than Lanier.

At the age of thirteen, Ryan felt a calling to the priesthood and entered a seminary where he was to remain until the age of twenty-two, when he was ordained. Initially a member of the Vincentian order, dedicated to missionary work among the rural poor, Father Ryan rebelled against the authority of his superiors, thus establishing a pattern that was to continue for the rest of his life. Exploiting a talent for preaching, he was eventually granted release from the society founded by St. Vincent de Paul and allowed to pursue a career as a parish priest and fundraiser.

Besides desiring greater personal independence, Ryan may have left the order because of its largely pro-Union stance. As war clouds loomed over the national horizon, Ryan found himself more and more at odds with his fellow Vincentians because of his Southern sympathies. His sectional loyalty manifested itself in a number of ways, including his refusal to use his full Christian name Abraham because of its association with Abraham Lincoln and his initial acceptance of slavery as a "scripturally sanctioned" practice. Ryan's rather uncompromising stance on both of these subjects was to soften over time, but throughout his life, he remained true to a largely sectionalist perspective.

Although he was assigned to a parish in Illinois when hostilities erupted between the North and the South, Ryan soon began making trips to

Confederate territory. His earliest excursions south were spent in a futile attempt to find the remains of his brother David, who had died in Confederate uniform in a military engagement in Kentucky. By 1864, however, he was spending time in Tennessee as an unofficial chaplain to various Rebel units.

Ironically enough, Ryan's greatest service to the Confederacy occurred not on the battlefield but after the war ended. In 1865, while assigned to a parish in Knoxville, he wrote perhaps his most famous poem, "The Conquered Banner." That poem and another eleven patriotic verses written over the next few years established his reputation as a versifier and solidified his position as one of the earliest proponents of the concept of the "lost cause," the contention that although the South had lost the war, the fight for states' rights had been an honorable one. The term appears as early as 1868 in Ryan's poem "Our Southern Dead": "Gather the sacred dust/of the warriors tried and true/who bore the flag of a Nation's trust/and fell in a cause, though lost, still just/and died for me and you."

That particular poem went to press when Father Ryan was in Augusta, serving as pastor of St. Patrick's Church and editor of a popular periodical entitled *Banner of the South*. Thus, in both the pulpit and in print, Ryan railed against Reconstruction and nurtured the cult of the lost cause. Although most of his patriotic poems were written before his Georgia residency, the time that Ryan spent as a newspaper editor in Augusta and as a public speaker, both in church and out, encompassed probably the two most influential years of his life.

While in Georgia, he gave some of his most significant speeches in Atlanta, arguing against what he perceived as the unjust penalties imposed upon the defeated South by the Radical Republicans then in control of the U.S. Congress. In his eyes, just as the Irish suffered under British imperialism, the South now lay helpless before northern despotism. During one such event in May 1869, no less a personage than Alexander Stephens, former vice president of the Confederacy, introduced Ryan to the overflow audience. Though his voice was "shrill," Ryan frequently won over his auditors through sheer histrionics; it is said, for example, that he would often feign illness at the beginning of an event, begging the forgiveness of those present for his incapacity, and then proceed to deliver a powerful two-hour address, made all the more compelling because it would appear that he had transcended his physical limitations in order to deliver his heartfelt message.

As an interesting side note, historians believe that Ryan loomed large in the collective memory of the Mitchell family because, it is conjectured, the grandparents of Margaret Mitchell heard one of Ryan's Atlanta speeches.

That is why Father Ryan makes an appearance in her famous novel *Gone with the Wind*.

Over time, however, as his reputation and notoriety grew, Ryan's superiors became more and more disquieted by his stridency; and despite his popularity with some of his parishioners in Augusta, he was asked to find a place outside the diocese in 1870. Consequently, Ryan moved to Alabama, where he continued to be lionized as a poet, particularly after the 1879 publication of *Father Ryan's Poems*, which eventually went through forty editions. He died in 1886 in a Franciscan monastery in Louisville, Kentucky, while on a speaking tour; he was buried in Mobile, Alabama.

The other two poets commemorated on Greene Street have more significant links to the city of Augusta than either Lanier or Ryan since both Paul Hamilton Hayne and James Ryder Randall found their final resting place in historic Magnolia Cemetery.

Hayne, who was born in Charleston, lost his home when the city was shelled by long-range Union artillery in 1862. After finding temporary lodgings with family in other parts of South Carolina, he moved to Grovetown, Georgia, where he lived in a modest cottage for more than twenty years. This structure was demolished in the 1950s. During his residency in the Augusta area, Hayne wrote many of his most notable poems and established a reputation as a literary critic and magazine editor. The Poets Monument features a stanza from one of the many sonnets by this most prolific writer; therein he claims that he would prefer of all fates the life of a "beggar basking by" the "radiant gate" of "song's immortal temple."

The fourth and final side of the Poets Monument calls attention to the life and work of James Ryder Randall, a Baltimore native most famous for having composed what became perhaps our country's most abidingly controversial state song, "Maryland, My Maryland." The twenty-two-year-old Randall was actually in Louisiana, teaching English at the college level, when he heard that some of the citizens of Baltimore had attacked Federal troops in 1861. Indeed, his friend Francis Ward was one of sixteen individuals, four soldiers and twelve civilians, killed in what became known in some circles as the Pratt Street Massacre. Many in Maryland, a slaveholding state at that time, were undoubtedly sympathetic to the idea of secession, and Randall penned "Maryland, My Maryland" to urge his fellow citizens to "avenge the patriotic gore that flecked the streets of Baltimore." His call proved ultimately ineffectual, however, because of President Lincoln's swift move to reinforce the military presence in the city and his jailing of suspected secessionists.

Set to the tune of "O Christmas Tree," Randall's poem eventually became a popular tune among Confederate troops during the war, and in 1939, the composition was adopted as Maryland's official state song. In the last few decades, however, repeated attempts have been made to change such lyrics as "She is not dead, nor deaf, nor dumb. Huzza! She spurns the Northern scum!" to something more palatable to contemporary listeners. All such legislative efforts to revise the state song have failed up to this point, with both sides of the issue—those wanting to preserve the song as an important remnant of the state's past and those wanting to modernize the lyrics—holding fast to their positions.

Sometimes called the "Tyrtaeus of the late war" after the ancient Greek lyric poet who is credited with having written poems that reinforced Spartan militarism, Randall wrote other compositions that were popular with Confederate soldiers, such as "The Battle Cry of the South," whose refrain reads as follows: "To arms! To arms! For the South needs help, and craven is he who flees—for ye have the sword of the Lion's Whelp, and the God of the Maccabees!" This equating of the Southern cause with that of Judah Maccabee and his four brothers and their descendants is interesting since Randall obviously wants to draw parallels to the ancient revolt of

Randall Monument, Greene Street, Augusta. *Tom Mack.*

the Maccabees against outside domination as part of their collective struggle to retain their own customs and way of life.

Denied military service due to a series of "lung hemorrhages," Randall served the Confederate cause with his pen, both as a poet and a correspondent. Eventually he settled in Augusta, where he worked as an editor and Washington correspondent for the *Augusta Chronicle*. He married Kate Hammond, a daughter of Colonel Marcus Hammond, whose family plantation Redcliffe across the Savannah River in Beech Island is now a South Carolina state park.

Randall's grave site in Magnolia Cemetery is modest compared to his monument on Greene Street in front of the Sacred Heart Cultural Center. Situated in the same section of the cemetery as the monument to Paul Hamilton Hayne, the Randall grave marker is a simple stone scroll with Randall's birth and death dates and the designation that he was the author of "My Maryland." The Greene Street memorial, however, features a full-length figure of Randall in a frock coat, his head bowed in contemplation; etched on the base is a stanza from the poem: "Better the fire upon thee roll, better the blade, the shot, the bowl, than crucifixion of the soul, Maryland! My Maryland!" Financed by the United Daughters of the Confederacy, the Randall Monument was placed in front of Sacred Heart, where the poet himself was once a member of the congregation.

So popular was the poem during his lifetime that even after he moved to Augusta, Randall continued to receive fan mail from across the country. It is not surprising, therefore, that he would name one of his daughters Maryland; she is buried next to her parents in the family plot in Magnolia Cemetery.

Established in 1817, Magnolia Cemetery, whose main entrance is on Third Street, joined the ranks of other parklike burial grounds popular in the nineteenth century not just as the final resting place of local citizens but also as a peaceful retreat from the hustle and bustle of daily life. Magnolia, for example, has fifteen lanes running east and west and two running north and south, crisscrossing sixty acres enclosed by the five-foot-high brick wall. On these grounds, city residents would sometimes stroll beneath the magnolia trees or even picnic on weekends beside the imposing mausoleums and elaborate monuments.

Among the most notable of those monuments are the two dedicated to Paul Hamilton Hayne and James Ryder Randall in what is now called Poet's Corner.

Chapter 17

1926: Author-Adventurer Uses Augusta Area as Home Base

In 2011, a Chicago-based camera dealer put up for auction a vintage Leica camera once owned by novelist Ernest Hemingway but presumably gifted to his friend Edison Marshall. Most literate Americans are familiar with Hemingway, whose adventurous personal life sometimes got more press than his fiction. The name "Edison Marshall" is far less familiar although in his lifetime, the Augusta-based author carved out a reputation for adventure, particularly in the arena of big-game hunting, rivaling that of Hemingway.

Like his more famous contemporary, Marshall was born in the Midwest. As a youngster in Indiana, he was given his first rifle, which he used to hunt rabbits in the Iroquois River Valley. From that moment in 1905, when he was eleven years old, Marshall asserts that he felt "the passion of the chase." It was a seductive call that he found irresistible for the rest of his days.

The family moved to Oregon two years later after his elderly father, an erstwhile newspaper publisher, decided to move to that state to become an orchardist; it was a boom time in the pear-growing business in the Rogue River Valley, but not everybody prospered. Borrowing against future crops, the Marshall family enterprise went bankrupt when a cold wave decimated their hoped-for harvest.

Partially to escape a gloomy homefront, young Edison—he was named after the inventor Thomas Edison—took up duck hunting. With money borrowed from his father, he was able to purchase a secondhand pump gun and a limited supply of shotgun shells; the family's financial struggles made it imperative that he make each shot count. Over time, Marshall came to consider ducks the "big game of small game," and even after a serious accident when he was seventeen—due to what he claimed was a defective safety device on his .22 rifle, he lost a thumb and the upper rim of his left ear—Marshall retained a lifelong fascination with these waterfowl.

When he was eighteen, the death of an uncle brought the family a much-needed inheritance to help pay off most of their debt and send young Marshall to college. During his freshman year at the University of Oregon, he sold his first short story to one of the most popular periodicals of the day, *Argosy*. The tale, which focused on how modern-day explorers discover a group of Neanderthals who have somehow survived in the far North, earned him $200. That successful submission gave Marshall the confidence he needed to plan a career as a professional writer. With his father's unfortunate example as a spur, he made a pledge: "I resolved never to be poor again, unless the gods made me so." His faith was not misplaced because he eventually earned a very comfortable living as a prolific contributor to magazines such as the *Saturday Evening Post*, *Field and Stream* and *Cosmopolitan* and a widely read novelist, whose long fiction first appeared in serialized form.

Several of his novels were adapted for the screen. The enormously popular *Benjamin Blake* (1941) became the basis for *Son of Fury* (1942), starring Tyrone Power as the titular protagonist who is cheated of his inheritance by his hot-tempered uncle played by George Sanders. Revenge is, however, ultimately his. Young Blake acquires a fortune in pearls during a sojourn on a South Seas island, and he uses the money gained by their sale to win back his title and lands. Breetholm, the Spanish colonial mansion that served as the Marshall family residence in Augusta from 1945 until after Marshall's death in 1967, was named for the English manor house that figures prominently in the novel.

The success of this book marked Marshall's transition from serialized novels to books published in a single volume. So proud was Marshall of his first venture in this category that he sued *McCall's* when one of its critics accused him of plagiarizing the plot of Emily Bronte's *Wuthering Heights*. Despite advice to the contrary, Marshall took his case to the courts, and he prevailed.

In 1953, a second film loosely based on *Benjamin Blake* was released. Entitled *Treasure of the Golden Condor*, this remake features a main character, played by Cornel Wilde, who is similarly disinherited by an unscrupulous uncle; but in this variation on the basic narrative, he decides to seek the money that he needs to reclaim his birthright by searching for treasure in Guatemala.

Breetholm, 704 Milledge Road, Augusta. *Reese Library Special Collections, Georgia Regents University, Augusta.*

Two more movie adaptations followed. *Yankee Pasha: The Adventures of John Starbuck* (1947) was translated into the film *Yankee Pasha* (1954), starring Jeff Chandler as an American fur trapper who rescues the woman he loves, played by Rhonda Fleming, from the sultan of Morocco after she is kidnapped by North African pirates on her way to France. Based on a twelfth-century poem about the legendary Norse raider Radnar Lodbrok, *The Viking* (1951) was made into a movie entitled *The Vikings* in 1958; therein two half brothers, Erik (Tony Curtis) and Einar (Kirk Douglas), fight to possess a princess played by Janet Leigh. So impressed was Douglas with the novel that in a private letter to Marshall, dated 1962, the actor-producer reminded the novelist that he was "more than interested" in any other fiction on which he might be working.

Marshall himself confessed that the "two great prizes" that he sought all his life were fame and fortune. The latter he craved to support his family—he met his wife, Agnes Flythe, when he was stationed at Camp Hancock in Augusta in 1918, and they set up housekeeping first in Oregon and then subsequently in Beaufort, South Carolina. To escape conflict with her mother-in-law and also to be closer to her own family, Agnes convinced her husband to return to the South.

The Beaufort residency, however, soon proved untenable due to Marshall's affair with a local woman. His quest for sexual gratification matched in some ways the lure of big-game hunting, and his life was punctuated by a string of affairs and a series of biennial hunting expeditions. This pattern persisted even after the family moved first to North Augusta to live at Seven Gables, a former hunting lodge that had been part of the Hampton Terrace Hotel complex, and then, after World War II, to "the hill" in Augusta.

Marshall's first forays into big-game hunting involved trips to the Far North. On his tenderfoot expedition to British Columbia, he bagged both moose and Osborn's caribou and carried the horns back home as trophies. It was also on these trips that he standardized his backpacking gear, trying never to exceed twenty pounds, including his gun, camera, binoculars, first-aid kit, reading material (he devoured the Sherlock Holmes narratives when he made his first trip to India) and candy. "I was a great candy eater on the trail," Marshall confessed in a volume devoted to his career as a big-game hunter; the book, entitled *The Heart of the Hunter* (1956), was dedicated to his friend Charles Swint, president of the Graniteville Company in Aiken County.

For his third trip to the "purifying cold" of the North, his destination was Alaska and his target the grizzly or "ursus horribilis." It took three shots, during a charge that began sixty feet away and ended at thirty, before he downed a six-hundred-pound male. The subsequent photo, which appeared in the *New York Times*, featured the bear's enormous bulk almost completely overwhelming the canoe used to transport the carcass back to camp.

Once he felt that he had proven his mettle with domestic game, Marshall set his sights on foreign climes. He justified these trips in part because he was convinced that he needed such experience to write convincing "animal stories." One of his proudest accomplishments in this regard was a tale entitled "The Elephant Remembers" about a Hindu boy who befriends an albino elephant; the tale won an O. Henry Prize.

For his first trip to Africa, Marshall had to set aside four months; there were no transatlantic flights at that time, and two months out of the four had to be reserved for the round-trip voyage by sea. Once in East Africa, he used Charles Cottar, a professional guide who hailed from Texas—Marshall had an aversion to the British during their years of empire; he found them arrogant and condescending—to engage in what he saw as a "test of hardihood, determination, self-control, and a certain skill." On this trip, he shot buffalo, boars, leopards and at least three lions. His moment of greatest fear, a "fright tempered and charged by awe," involved his confrontation with a rhinoceros, which he described as a "brown relic of the antediluvian age." The beast was first sighted at a distance of one hundred yards in a field of "close-growing thorn." Marshall made his first shot but, in fumbling for a second cartridge, discovered a hole in the pocket of his leather jacket where he stored his shells. Luckily, the gun, a .405 Winchester, favored by President Teddy Roosevelt in his own big-game expeditions, had three more rounds in the chamber.

After his first visit to Africa, Marshall went to French Indochina, in quest primarily of the wild water buffalo, whose wide, bow-shaped horns were prized as big-game trophies. On this trip, he was introduced to his "first true jungle" with its "intermeshing foliage overhead" through which sunlight fell in "spots and splashes." He also killed his first tiger.

Two years later, he was in Laos and Thailand, and two years after that, when he was not quite forty years of age, he made a long-anticipated voyage to India, still under British rule. Eschewing the mode of vice-regal shoots wherein hundreds of beaters drive the quarry to the hunters, Marshall hired a Eurasian guide to organize his own elephant-mounted safari. Perched on a stiff mattress tied around the belly of the elephant and traveling at roughly four miles per hour, the short, bespectacled author set out in search of Indian bison and what had now become his favorite prey: the tiger.

Edison Marshall in Africa with a dead leopard. *Reese Library Special Collections, Georgia Regents University, Augusta.*

For a souvenir, he craved the tiger's brilliantly colored fur, what he called the "ultimate Golden Fleece." Despite the fact that he was mounted on an elephant with a "nervous temperament," Marshall achieved a great deal of success regarding his objective. Unlike the carnivores of Africa, which were hunted largely for sport, the Bengal tiger was frequently a menace to village life. The big cats often raided the fields, killing domestic livestock and even humans.

By his second trip to India in 1937, Marshall had earned the sobriquet "Big American Hunter Master." Indeed, on that expedition alone, he bagged four tigers, including some so notorious that the natives had given them names, such as the "Ogress," the "White-Faced One" and the "Grandfather of Tigers." Although by this time in his career he was happy to acknowledge that he was a "writer of some small note," Marshall was most pleased to be acknowledged as a big-game hunter.

As he got older, however, Marshall found that he could no longer cope with the rigors of a hunt for tigers or rogue elephants, so he contented himself with safaris closer to his Augusta home and the quarry that he first chose as a boy: ducks. He was accustomed, in his later years, to hunting or fishing at least three days a week. He credited living in Augusta with providing the time and relative isolation, "avoiding New York, Hollywood, and other pressures," that he needed to maintain the lifestyle he craved. He died in 1967 in Augusta.

In the final analysis, nothing—not his popular success as a writer nor the many sexual conquests enumerated in his unpublished autobiography—could fill Edison Tesla Marshall with as much joy as hunting big game with all of its attendant "quickening of all the senses and the strengthening of the life force."

Chapter 18

1938: The Godfather of Soul Gets His Start in Augusta

About a year and a half before his death on Christmas 2006, James Brown was honored by Augusta, his adopted city, with the dedication of a statue in his image. Situated in a plaza carved from the median on Broad Street between Eighth and what is now James Brown Boulevard, the nearly life-sized rendering of Brown was created by John B. Savage, a local surgeon and sculptor, who wanted to depict the legendary performer in a dignified pose not unlike those reserved for politicians and other public figures.

According to several firsthand reports, however, Brown was not comfortable with that approach. Instead, he wanted to be remembered with a big smile on his face as if imbued with the joy he felt on stage, performing before an enthusiastic audience. As a consequence, the statue unveiled on May 6, 2005, captures a broadly grinning entertainer in a vested suit, covered by a cape like the ones placed on his shoulders near the end of his physically exhausting programs. With both hands, Brown holds a microphone stand tilted slightly as if he has just finished a song and is now basking in appreciative applause.

James Brown started life far from the international spotlight he was eventually to enjoy. Born in what he himself described as a "one-room shack" near Barnwell, South Carolina, in 1933, he lived alone with his father, Joseph, in the countryside after his parents split up when he was four. At the age of five or six, Brown moved to Augusta to live with his great-aunt Minnie, who had taken up residence with another relative—Brown identified her as yet another aunt—Handsome Washington, popularly called Honey.

The James Brown statue, Broad Street, Augusta. *Tom Mack*.

Honey became a major figure in Brown's early life, providing him with a roof over his head—prior to this point he and his father had lived without windows, plumbing and electricity—and offering him a role model on survival. Honey did everything she could to make ends meet; she converted her residence, a former funeral home on Twiggs Street, into a boardinghouse wherein she also hosted a gambling operation, sold moonshine and ran a string of prostitutes. Her establishment flourished for a time in what was then called "the Terry," short for Verdery's Territory, the south end of town to which emancipated slaves flocked after the Civil War. It might be argued that this African American neighborhood, deprived of the urban amenities accorded Augusta's white residents, had not changed appreciably since the end of that momentous conflict; the streets were still mostly unpaved thoroughfares of clay and sand.

Even as a child, Brown took an active part in the family business, particularly when the city became flooded with servicemen during World War II. To add to the household income, Brown canvassed the streets for customers for his aunt's assorted services, especially the commercialization of female companionship. He also shined shoes and made tentative steps toward a career in entertainment.

An older cousin taught him a few dance steps in the mode of what Brown himself called "country buck dancing," a variation on clogging, and he would make nickels and dimes performing on the street. He also taught himself how to play several musical instruments, including the piano, guitar and drums. At the age of eleven, Brown entered his first amateur competition at the old Lenox Theater, which was eventually demolished in 1978; thanks in part to the sheer volume of his vocalizing, he won first place.

Poverty, the abandonment of his parents and the lack of suitable adult supervision impelled him, from an early age, to fend largely for himself; he dropped out of school in the fifth grade at the age of ten. Ironically, it was, he himself argued, because of the fact that he had no clothes appropriate for school that he began to engage in criminal activity, confined largely to what he called "stealing." He began by appropriating hubcaps but gradually advanced to taking things from parked automobiles. The lure was largely financial, but there was also an element of adventure in his larceny. Brown claims to have stolen only from those who already had more than they needed—in this case, whites—and never from those on the bottom of the socioeconomic ladder. He also took some pride in being able to outwit the police, sometimes jumping into the canal to evade capture and other times outrunning members of the constabulary as they chased him down Broad Street.

Eventually, however, Brown's luck ran out, and he was apprehended at the age of fifteen and charged with four counts of breaking and entering (automobiles). He turned sixteen while in jail, so he was eventually tried as an adult and sentenced to a term of between eight and sixteen years. Such was the nature of the judicial system at that time that he had no real legal defense—he did not even meet his court-appointed attorney until the day of his trial.

Despite the harsh and disproportionate sentence, jail may have proven to be the salvation of James Brown. After two years at the Georgia Juvenile Training Institute in Rome, the whole facility was moved to Toccoa. During this period in his life, two of Brown's talents came in handy: he could box—as a left-handed boxer, he seemed to have an advantage over those who wanted to pick a fight—and he could sing. Given the nickname Music Box because of his devotion to gospel music, Brown was eventually made a trusty after earning the respect and protection of the warden, Walter Matthews, who later became a lifelong mentor.

It was Matthews who offered Brown parole five years into his sentence. He was forbidden to return to Augusta; as a requirement of that release, even after he started to make a name for himself as a performer, Brown had to ask permission of the Richmond County district attorney to play a show in Augusta, and even then, he could not stay in the city more than twenty-four hours. However, if he could find a job in Toccoa, he would be released. Brown found part-time work as a janitor in a local plastics factory and a handyman at an Oldsmobile dealership; he also moonlighted in 1952–53 as a member of the Flames, the earliest incarnation of what would later become the Famous Flames. Their break-through hit, "Please, Please, Please," was a million-selling single in 1956; it reached number five on the rhythm and blues chart.

In his 1986 autobiography, Brown mentions some of the influences that he drew upon in the development of what was to be his standard stage performance. Claiming that much of his public persona "came out of the church," Brown was inspired by some of the charismatic preachers whom he had witnessed as a young boy, particularly their dramatic vocalizations and body language. He was particularly intrigued by the showmanship of Charles "Sweet Daddy" Grace, whose United House of Prayer for All People attracted scores of congregants; after carefully orchestrated street parades on Wrightsboro Road, the self-styled bishop would sermonize in suits made of money, his flamboyant garb concealed by a cape until the moment when he would be fully revealed to optimum dramatic effect. Thus, some biographers credit Daddy Grace and others cite the pro wrestler Gorgeous George as the inspiration for Brown's decision to have a garment placed over his shoulders at the end of his performance; in the beginning, he used a simple robe bought off the rack, but as he became more successful, he graduated to capes of his own design.

In the early days, his stage show, replete with singers, dancers and instrumentalists, was likened to that of Little Richard. Indeed, both men had a friendly rivalry over which of their shows could be more theatrical; and when the latter retired temporarily from rock-and-roll in 1957, Brown took over much of Richard's schedule of shows in Georgia, which was then part of what was called the "chitlin' circuit."

Like Little Richard, Brown was always a sharp dresser. Perhaps memories of his being sent home from school as a child because of inadequate and inappropriate clothing left a residual sting. But there can be no doubt that he eventually overcompensated for the wardrobe deficiencies of his youth; at the height of his career in the 1960s and '70s, for instance, he could boast a wardrobe of up to five hundred suits and three hundred pairs of shoes.

The stylish clothes were a large part of the James Brown persona; there was also the big smile and the carefully crafted hairdo—what he himself called "fried and to the side." In his 1986 autobiography, Brown claimed that all a man really needed was his teeth and his hair.

Brown's artistic and commercial success, however, remained largely a southern phenomenon until one of his live performances was captured and released on record in 1963. That recording, *Live at the Apollo*, gave a national audience a taste of the infectious energy generated by Brown on stage, and the album went to number two on the Billboard chart. Most of the tracks on this album are characteristic of the artist's mature style, a rhythmic counterbalance between largely improvisational lead vocals, partially sung and partially spoken, and hard-hitting, pulsating instrumentation.

The rest is history. Over a career spanning five decades, Brown made the Billboard Hot 100 singles chart ninety-four times. His repertoire of over eight hundred songs included such popular titles as "Papa's Got a Brand New Bag," "I Got You (I Feel Good)," "It's a Man's, Man's, Man's World" and "Living in America."

However, even as an international audience elevated him to the status of a pop superstar, Brown faced personal challenges. His problems with the law followed him into adulthood and the period of his greatest fame. Significant tax problems surfaced in the mid-1970s, and many of Brown's initial investments he lost principally as a result of alleged tax irregularities: a string of radio stations, including WRDW in Augusta; a chain of soul food restaurants, dubbed Gold Platter; and, within a span of five years, first his Augusta residence on Walton Way and then (temporarily) his home in Beech Island, South Carolina.

More serious legal difficulties followed in the 1980s with a series of arrests for drug possession and domestic abuse that garnered headlines around the world. Brown's most serious altercation occurred in September 1988 when he was sentenced to six years in prison after brandishing a weapon in a building next door to the Broad Street headquarters of his Man's World Enterprises and then leading local police on a two-state, high-speed chase, from Augusta to Aiken County and then back to Augusta. Assigned to the minimum-security Lower Savannah Community Work Center, Brown was given work-release privileges, granted supervised leave to counsel young people under the auspices of the Aiken and Barnwell Counties Community Action Commission. He earned parole after two and a half years.

Some might argue that rather than offering advice to others, Brown himself needed counseling. Indeed, after years of denial, he finally admitted in his second autobiography, this one published in 2005, that he had for some time been struggling with "hard drugs." Thus, the man honored by Governor Jimmy Carter in 1972 for his public work regarding the dangers of drug abuse himself became a victim.

All in all, James Brown offers a study in contradiction. A strong advocate of African American capitalism, he built an entertainment empire only to lose most of it due to poor financial management. A consistent advocate of self-empowerment, he fell prey to his own personal demons, particularly in his troubled relationship with all four of his wives and his evolving dependence on controlled substances. Possessed of a quick temper and accused at times of behavior demeaning to his employees, Brown was at key moments in his public life a peacemaker, especially in Augusta in May 1970 when riots broke out, sparked by the death of an African American youth in the same jail that once housed Brown himself. "Don't save face—save your city" was part of the message that Brown broadcast on his radio station and on other local media outlets.

In the final analysis, however, it is not the man but his musical legacy that will be remembered most. No matter how much his personal life might flicker and dim, his musical star remained bright. Brown was inducted into the Rock and Roll Hall of Fame in 1986, he received a Lifetime Achievement Grammy in 1992 and he was a Kennedy Center Honoree in 2003.

This international recognition was matched by official acknowledgments on the homefront. In 1993, part of Ninth Street in Augusta was renamed James Brown Boulevard; and in 2006, the year of his death from pneumonia in an Atlanta hospital at the age of seventy-three, the Augusta–Richmond County Civic Center was renamed the James Brown Arena. That entertainment complex became the site of a four-hour "home-going" service just a few days after the death of "Soul Brother Number One." In attendance were pop superstar Michael Jackson, who claimed that Brown was his "greatest inspiration," and Al Sharpton, who asserted that "nobody started lower and went higher than James Brown."

The James Brown statue on Broad Street, however, still remains the most popular tourist site associated with the Godfather of Soul. Brown asked city officials that it not be placed on a pedestal so that his fans could pose with the figure. Brown saw himself as a man of the people, and he wanted his sculpted image to be perpetually accessible.

On a plaque near the statue, James Brown is extolled as an individual who "thrilled millions with his hit recordings and electrifying recordings." Indeed, despite all the laudable attempts by municipal authorities to commemorate his connection to his adopted city, Brown's music will ultimately be his greatest monument.

Chapter 19

1940: Author-Crusader Fights Political Corruption in the Inter-War Period

In the 1947 novel *The Lightwood Tree*, the protagonist, a high school history teacher named George Cliatt, is confronted with a moral dilemma. He must choose between maintaining job security and taking a stand against injustice. Set in Augusta, Georgia, which is called in the book Fredericksville (a probable reference to Princess Augusta's ill-fated husband), the narrative is loosely based on real-life events during a single week in 1942.

While our country was at war against global fascism, there was an autocratic oligarchy very much in charge of local affairs. For nearly a quarter of a century, the so-called Cracker Party had assumed a stranglehold on municipal government, purchasing the loyalty of Augusta's voters by a host of small favors and exhorting kickbacks from public employees. Led by "Boss" John B. Kennedy, the unelected public safety commissioner who controlled the police and fire departments, the Crackers imposed one-party rule on the city.

What finally sparked a citizens' revolt was the arrest of one man, Bridges Evans, who had dared to criticize publicly the city administration during the course of a high school football game. As the title of Fleming's novel suggests—the term "lightwood" is a southern expression for any wood used as kindling—this single overstepping of legal authority on the part of the city's ruling party, a move that the *Augusta Chronicle* called reminiscent of "Gestapo tactics," lit the fire that resulted in a toppling of the Cracker Party at the hands of a reformist citizenry.

One of the leading lights of that movement, labeled the Augusta Citizens Union, was its treasurer and the author of *The Lightwood Tree*, Berry Fleming. Like his fictional character George Cliatt, Fleming, whose own Georgia roots ran deep, was forced to become involved in civic affairs after his return to Augusta in 1933.

Born and raised on Greene Street and educated at Richmond Academy (where the fictional George Cliatt was on the faculty), Fleming graduated in 1922 from Harvard University and moved in 1923 to New York City, where he contributed to a number of national periodicals. Fleming's return to the city of his birth was necessitated in part by his mother's illness and in part by his desire for subject matter. He came to the conclusion, he told others, that he needed "more direct experience with American life than [he] seemed to get in New York" and that he had only one choice: to be a "Southern novelist or no novelist at all."

Thanks to his column "The Watchtower," which appeared regularly in the *Augusta Chronicle*, Fleming became an influential voice in the town of his birth. National prominence came later with the publication of a series of novels, including his most popular novel and Book-of-the-Month Club selection *Colonel Effingham's Raid*. This book covers some of the same territory as *The Lightwood Tree* in that it also deals with a grass-roots effort to combat the political corruption of the Cracker Party.

In this 1943 novel and its subsequent 1946 cinematic translation, a retired military man, Colonel Effingham (played by Charles Coburn in the film), uses his popular newspaper column to take on city hall when he discovers that the current mayor and his cronies have plans to tear down the historic courthouse while simultaneously lining their own pockets. To some extent, Colonel Effingham's journalistic career and his interest in historic preservation mirror Fleming's own initiatives—he helped form the Richmond County Historical Society the same year that the movie was released. Sadly, however, neither the success of the book and film nor the establishment of the historical society could forestall the eventual destruction of the landmark that inspired all that attention: the splendid Richmond County Courthouse, erected circa 1821 and enlarged in 1892 but torn down in 1957.

In an unpublished biographical sketch that Fleming wrote in 1947 as part of the "twenty-fifth anniversary report of the 1922 class at Harvard," he directly referenced how his political activism was sparked by news that the "local political machine" was planning without popular support to raze the historic courthouse. It seemed at the time, Fleming asserted, that "democracy needed some defenders on Main Street." Thus, according to his

Above: Fleming's childhood home, 453 Greene Street, Augusta. *Library of Congress*.

Left: Fleming Home, built circa 1912 and the author's primary residence from 1940 until his death, 2242 Pickens Road, Augusta. *Tom Mack*.

Old Richmond County Courthouse, built in 1821 and remodeled in 1892. *Library of Congress.*

own account, he spent the next four years in a whirlwind of "ballot boxes, registration lists, polling places, meetings, canvassings, shoulders lukewarm-to-cold, stares icy-to-glacial, warnings and threats and insults, strange friends and stranger enemies, unexpected help and even more unexpected failures to help."

The efforts of the Augusta Citizens Union eventually bore fruit with the electoral defeat of the Cracker Party in 1946. As an interesting side note, "Boss" Kennedy met his end in 1951 at the hands of his own wife, who shot him six times during an argument in the family home. According to a report in the *Chicago Tribune*, the shooting was in response to his hitting her when he discovered that she had taken a job in a local "beer parlor."

Fleming himself fared much better than the target of his civic ire; up until his death in 1989 at the age of ninety, he remained a major cultural figure in his native city and state. He is buried in the Fleming plot in Summerville Cemetery amid the grave sites of other members of his family. Most are marked by flat, cross-shaped stones etched with quotes from literary figures

Left: Berry Fleming, circa 1940. *Reese Library Special Collections, Georgia Regents University, Augusta.*

Right: The grave site of Berry Fleming, Summerville Cemetery, Augusta. *Tom Mack.*

such as John Keats, Henry David Thoreau and Dylan Thomas. Berry Fleming's gravestone identifies him as a "man of vision who valued words and used them well."

The marker also bears a quote from the poem "Academic Discourse" by Wallace Stevens, a set of lines sometimes taken out of context and interpreted in isolation as an assertion of the poet's power to refocus the attention of his listeners on those things that might otherwise be ignored: "Let the poet on his balcony speak and the sleepers in their sleep shall move, waken, and watch the moonlight on their floors." In similar fashion, Berry Fleming tried in his novels to get his fellow Augustans to observe what was happening around them in the city where he grew up and spent the major part of his life as both a witness and interpreter.

Chapter 20

1945: FACING RACIAL AND GENDER-BASED CHALLENGES, SOPRANO MAINTAINS HER "SINGING SPIRIT"

The basic trajectory of Jessye Norman's extraordinary life is known to lovers of serious music around the world: how a young woman from a middle-class Augusta family found operatic stardom in Europe and became an international phenomenon. Yet under the glamorous veneer lies a tale of one individual's indefatigable determination to stay true to her inner voice.

Born in 1945, Norman was one of five children raised by parents prominent in the black community. Her father, Silas, was a branch manager of the North Carolina Life Insurance Company, perhaps the largest African American–owned business in the country at that time, and a deacon at Mount Calvary Baptist Church; her mother, Janie, was a homemaker and educator. Music was part of family life. The women in the family sang around the house and in church. No one, however, had any particular attraction to opera; that was Norman's own discovery, listening to radio broadcasts of productions of the Metropolitan Opera on a radio in her bedroom. Questioned as to how one so young could comprehend what she heard on the airwaves, Norman credited Milton Cross, the voice of the Met for forty-three years, for kindling her childhood imagination.

Eventually, she graduated from listening to performing. As a student at Lucy Laney High School, she sang her first aria, the hauntingly beautiful "My Heart at Thy Sweet Voice" from Camille Saint-Saens's *Samson and Delilah*. She was fortunate to find encouragement in her community, and she was not without role models. In fact, one of her earliest inspirations, the soprano Marian Anderson, indirectly provided a path forward for the young woman from Augusta. At the age of fifteen, Norman traveled to Philadelphia to enter the Marian Anderson Vocal Competition. Established in 1943 by the groundbreaking star whose 1939 recital on the steps of the Lincoln Memorial was one of the landmarks of the early civil rights movement, the competition gave recognition to many talented young singers until its discontinuation in 1976. Although Norman did not win a prize, her vocal promise attracted the attention of the music faculty at Howard University, and she was eventually offered a full-tuition scholarship to study music at that private, historically black institution.

From there, the rest is history. More education followed; she attended a summer institute at the Peabody Conservatory and earned a master's degree at the University of Michigan. Finally, on the strength of her first-place award at the Bavarian Radio International Music Competition in 1969, Norman got a three-year contract with the Berlin Opera, and her professional career was launched.

Still, as her 2014 autobiography makes clear, the road to success was not without its obstacles. As a youngster and later as an adult, she faced challenges posed by both restrictive gender expectations and racial bias. The former she first encountered in her own family and community when she came to envy from an early age the relative freedom of her brothers and the gender-specific bonding experiences they enjoyed with their father, especially the early morning fishing expeditions in which she yearned to play a part. Furthermore, at the age of thirteen, Norman took a stand in support of personal choice by declaring what she called a "one-girl war against home economics." Unfairly assigned to a class with sewing needles and spatulas—she wanted to take industrial arts with the boys—Norman resisted the lesson plans repeatedly, incurring the displeasure of the principal on one memorable occasion when she refused to participate in preparing a breakfast for members of the school's male population.

Even in her professional career, Norman resisted conformity to the existing system, questioning, for example, the tradition, in some European venues, of paying male performers higher salaries than their female counterparts. Perhaps more insidious, however, was the sly criticism that she occasionally endured regarding body image. Even in the world of opera, where voice trumps all, social standards of physical attractiveness intrude, and Norman has faced the periodic accusation that her height and weight—what Morley Safer described as her "majestic proportions" in a 1991 *60 Minutes* broadcast—have kept her from performing certain key roles. Although she has repeatedly asserted that her "dress size" has never stopped her from doing what she wanted to do, the charge lingers.

Additional barriers have been imposed by race. Norman carries with her to this day many memories of growing up in the segregated South. There was, for example, the time that her father took the family to catch a glimpse of President Dwight D. Eisenhower leaving Reid Memorial Presbyterian Church, where he was a frequent congregant; waiting on the sidewalk was their only option since people of color were barred from entering that particular Walton Way house of worship at that time.

Later, in the 1960s, Norman herself would join other African American students in bus and lunch counter protests in downtown Augusta. On one such occasion, she feared for her life. While protesting a local supermarket's policy of using African Americans in menial positions only, members of the sidewalk picketers were almost run down by an irate motorist.

During this time of political and social change, her parents encouraged the involvement of their children in the collective fight for justice. Her elder brother Silas Jr. was a leading force in the NAACP's youth chapter at Paine College, and in that capacity, he once escorted Dr. Martin Luther King Jr. during a portion of his 1962 visit to the city to speak at Tabernacle Baptist Church.

Long after forced integration in this country and subsequent to her establishing her own significant professional identity, Jessye Norman has felt the latent sting of racism. Sometimes, as she recounts in her autobiography, she has suffered at the hands of insensitive hotel workers who have questioned why a woman of color should be staying at their luxury hostelry; other times, individuals in the musical profession have been the cause of painful encounters. Once, after she had mentioned to a noted British conductor that the Scott Joplin piece they were rehearsing was in the wrong tempo, he presumably rejoined, "Well, it's your music. You must know."

Still, in her distinguished career, Norman herself has done much to break down racial barriers. Her first role at the Deutsche Oper Berlin, for example, was Elisabeth in Richard Wagner's *Tannhauser*. This role is normally cast with a blonde Nordic-looking soprano, so Norman broke the mold as soon as she stepped on stage in her December 1969 operatic debut. What is more, she has continued over her long career to triumph against type, such as when, draped in the French tricolors, she sang "La Marseillaise" to an international television audience on the 200th anniversary of the French Revolution on July 14, 1989. For an African American female to be singing the French national anthem ran completely counter to the traditional image of Marianne, the

Jessye Norman Amphitheater, Riverwalk, Augusta. *Tom Mack.*

female personification of the French Republic immortalized in Eugene Delacroix's famous painting *Liberty Leading the People*. Yet over and over again, Norman has carved out a career that defies expectations, particularly preconceived notions about race. "Pigeonholing," Norman once said, "is only interesting to pigeons."

Through it all, Jessye Norman has retained the "singing spirit" passed down from mother to daughter in her family. The citizens of the city of Augusta remain justly proud of their native daughter, dedicating to her the 1,800-seat outdoor amphitheater on the Riverwalk and establishing in 2003 the Jessye Norman School of the Arts.

BIBLIOGRAPHY

Andrews, Matthew Page, ed. *The Poems of James Ryder Randall.* New York: Tandy-Thomas, 1910.

Beagle, Donald Robert, and Bryan Giemza. *Poet of the Lost Cause: A Life of Father Ryan.* Knoxville: University of Tennessee Press, 2008.

Benet, Stephen Vincent. *John Brown's Body.* 1927. Reprint, New York: Holt, Rinehart and Winston, 1955.

Benson, Susan Williams, ed. *Berry Benson's Civil War Book.* Athens: University of Georgia Press, 1962.

Berry Fleming: Augusta Artist and Author. Augusta, GA: Morris Museum of Art, 2000.

Bragg, C.L., et al. *Never for Want of Powder: The Confederate Powder Works in Augusta, Georgia.* Columbia: University of South Carolina Press, 2007.

Brown, James. *The Godfather of Soul.* New York: Macmillan, 1986.

———. *I Feel Good: A Memoir of a Life of Soul.* New York: New American Library, 2005.

Brown, Russell K. *To the Manner Born: The Life of General William H.T. Walker.* Athens: University of Georgia Press, 1994.

Butt, Archibald. *Taft and Roosevelt: The Intimate Letters of Archie Butt, Military Aide.* 2 vols. Garden City, NY: Doubleday, 1930.

Cashin, Edward J. *A Confederate Legend: Sergeant Berry Benson in War and Peace.* Macon, GA: Mercer University Press, 2008.

———. *General Sherman's Girl Friend and Other Stories about Augusta.* Columbia, SC: Bryan, 1992.

————. *The Story of Augusta*. Augusta, GA: Richmond County Board of Education, 1980.

Chesnut, Mary Boykin. *A Diary from Dixie*. Edited by Ben Ames Williams. Boston: Houghton Mifflin, 1949.

Corley, Florence Fleming. *Confederate City: Augusta, Georgia 1860–1865*. Columbia: University of South Carolina Press, 1960.

Coulter, E. Merton. *Wormsloe: Two Centuries of a Georgia Family*. Athens: University of Georgia Press, 1955.

Crouch, Tom D. *The Bishop's Boys: A Life of Wilbur and Orville Wright*. New York: Norton, 1989.

De-la-Noy, Michael. *The King Who Never Was: The Story of Frederick, Prince of Wales*. London: Peter Owen, 1996.

Fenton, Charles A. *Stephen Vincent Benet: The Life and Times of an American Man of Letters, 1898–1943*. New Haven, CT: Yale University Press, 1958.

Fleming, Berry. *The Lightwood Tree*. Philadelphia: J.B. Lippincott, 1947.

Floyd, Silas Xavier. *Life of Charles T. Walker*. 1902. Reprint, New York: Negro Universities Press, 1969.

George, Nelson, and Alan Leeds, eds. *The James Brown Reader: Fifty Years of Writing about the Godfather of Soul*. New York: Penguin, 2008.

Hayne, Paul Hamilton. *Antebellum Charleston: The Southern Bivouac*. 1885. Reprint, Columbia: University of South Carolina Press, 1978.

Howard, Fred. *Wilbur and Orville: A Biography of the Wright Brothers*. New York: Knopf, 1987.

Izzo, David Garrett, and Lincoln Konkle, eds. *Stephen Vincent Benet: Essays on His Life and Work*. Jefferson, NC: McFarland, 2003.

Lukowski, Jerzy, and Hubert Zawardzki. *A Concise History of Poland*. Cambridge, UK: University of Cambridge Press, 2002.

Mack, Tom. *Circling the Savannah*. Charleston, SC: The History Press, 2009.

————. *Hidden History of Aiken County*. Charleston, SC: The History Press, 2012.

Marshall, Edison. *Benjamin Blake*. New York: Literary Guild, 1941.

————. *The Heart of the Hunter*. New York: McGraw-Hill, 1956.

Moore, Rayburn. *A Man of Letters in the Nineteenth-Century South: Selected Letters of Paul Hamilton Hayne*. Baton Rouge: Louisiana State University Press, 1982.

Norman, Jessye. *Stand Up Straight and Sing!* Boston: Houghton Mifflin Harcourt, 2014.

O'Connell, David. *Furl that Banner: The Life of Abram J. Ryan, Poet-Priest of the South*. Macon, GA: Mercer University Press, 2006.

Rowland, A. Ray, and Helen Callahan. *Yesterday's Augusta*. Miami, FL: E.A. Seemann, 1976.

Sargent, Mildred Crow. *William Few, a Founding Father*. New York: Vantage Press, 2004.

Stroud, Parry. *Stephen Vincent Benet*. New York: Twayne, 1962.

Sullivan, James. *The Hardest Working Man: How James Brown Saved the Soul of America*. New York: Penguin, 2008.

Summer, Penelope. "A Bibliographical Study of the Novels and Novellas of Berry Fleming." Thesis, University of South Carolina, 1993.

Tucker, Edward. *Richard Henry Wilde: His Life and Selected Poems*. Athens: University of Georgia Press, 1966.

Vivian, Frances. *A Life of Frederick, Prince of Wales, 1707–1751: A Connoisseur of the Arts*. Lewiston, NY: Edwin Mellen Press, 2006.

Watson, Thomas E. *The Life and Times of Thomas Jefferson*. New York: Appleton, 1903.

———. *The Roman Catholic Hierarchy*: *The Deadliest Menace to American Liberties and Christian Civilization*. Thomson, GA: Jeffersonian Publishing Co., 1915.

Woodward, C. Vann. *Tom Watson: Agrarian Rebel*. London: Oxford University Press, 1963.

Wright, Nathalia. "The Italian Son of Richard Henry Wilde." *Georgia Historical Quarterly* 43, no. 4 (1959): 419–27.

About the Author

Dr. Mack with the Confederate obelisk-chimney and Sibley Mill, Augusta. *Michael Budd.*

Dr. Tom Mack began his career as a member of the English Department at the University of South Carolina–Aiken in 1976. For his "enviable record of teaching excellence as well as outstanding performance in scholarship and public service," the USC Board of Trustees awarded him the prestigious Carolina Trustee Professorship in 2008. His classroom work has been recognized by his receipt of the Amoco Foundation Outstanding Teaching Award and the 2010 SC Center for the Book Award in Teaching. In the scholarly arena, he has published to date over 100 articles on American literature and cultural history and four books, including *Circling the Savannah* and *Hidden History of Aiken County* (The History Press), *A Shared Voice* (Lamar University Press) and *The South Carolina Encyclopedia Guide to South Carolina Writers* (University of South Carolina Press). He is the founding editor of the *Oswald Review*, the first international refereed journal of undergraduate research in the discipline of English (www.scholarcommons.sc.edu). Since 1990, Mack has also contributed a weekly column to the *Aiken Standard*—over 1,300 columns to date devoted to the arts and humanities. In recognition of his work as a cultural critic, he received the 2013 Media Arts Award from the Greater Augusta Arts Council. Dr. Mack has also served as chair of the Board of Governors of the South Carolina Academy of Authors, the organization responsible for managing the state's literary hall of fame (www.scacademyofauthors.org); in the latter capacity, he is credited with having revitalized the academy's mission and enhanced its profile in the state. In addition, Mack currently serves on the boards of the Humanities Council SC and the Historic Aiken Foundation, as well as the advisory council of the Etherredge Center for the Performing Arts. He is also a member of the Authors Club of Augusta. For his many contributions to the cultural life of Aiken and South Carolina as a whole, Dr. Mack was presented with the Governor's Award in the Humanities in 2014.